Unlocking the Magic of Leadership

5 Keys to Inspiring Yourself,
Empowering Others and
Driving Extraordinary Results

Summer Jelinek

Former Walt Disney World Leader and
Disney Institute Facilitator

For more information, email summer@summerjelinek.com
ISBN: 979-8-89109-599-1 (paperback)
ISBN: 979-8-89109-615-8 (hardcover)
ISBN: 979-8-89109-614-1 (ebook)

To my husband, Miles Jelinek III,
for always believing enough for the both of us.
LYLM

TABLE OF CONTENTS

INTRODUCTION

Kindergarten had been a year of learning and growing. My first year as a student. It was a year of making friends and learning that some kids are different than others, some could be convinced more easily than others. Some kids had to be... guided with a little heavier of a hand. One of these kids, let's call him Alex, had refused to fall in with the rest of the kids when I was passing out suggestions as to what we should play. When he refused to fall in, I figured it would be easier to give him a nudge, than to spend time trying to convince him. So I beat him up. That was the path my kindergarten self took.

Fast forward to my first day of first grade and there is Alex, standing at the door of our first grade class, crying. Well, screaming really, that he wasn't going to come into the room unless I wasn't there. I didn't see what the big deal was. If he would just listen to me, everything would go much smoother for him. I am assuming the adults took care of it because he didn't come back to the class.

You see, I would like to say I was born a natural leader, but that would be inaccurate. Instead of being a leader, I was the bully on the playground. Where other kids could use things like influence, I was more efficient. I used threats of pain. Was this the correct way? Of course not. Even at such an early age, I could see that the kids that used influence instead of coercion had an easier time of it. The other kids wanted to play with them. They wanted to be friends. This was frustrating and confusing for me, and very lonely.

I quickly became focused on what was different between the other kids and myself. What made some kids the life of the party, others the bully, and others the outsiders. From the outside in, it felt like a magic trick that they knew, and I didn't. As I grew older, I stopped using violence and threats, but still found applying influence extraordinarily hard. I wanted the other kids to like me. I wanted to be a part of their world, but it just felt like they had a superpower that I was lacking.

When I went to college in my mid twenties, I had explored different careers and industries. I was a little older than the average student, but not necessarily any wiser. I didn't know what I wanted to be when I grew up, but I knew I wanted to be in charge, so I went to school for business management. That was where I first began using my super power– learning vast amounts of information and pulling the thread of commonality through them, to understand what we know as management and leadership. From that moment on, the companies that I worked for, the coaches that I chose, the leaders that I followed, the research I focused on, were all done with a very specific purpose. This was to understand what made some people worth following and others not. I wanted to understand the "magic trick" that became apparent on the playground, and continued to frustrate me throughout my life.

I uncovered during this time the M.A.G.I.C. model, a five step system that the most successful leaders take to create an environment in which individuals choose to follow them.

M - Manage Yourself First
A - Align Your Purpose
G - Galvanize Your Employees
I - Inspire Yourself and Others
C - Control Your Chaos

An important note here: all of these leaders were extremely different. Some were extroverted, some introverted, some optimistic, some pessimistic, some led from the front while others led from the back. It was less about individual personality traits and more about what they did with them. What this means is that every individual who chooses to take on the mantle and responsibility of leadership has the ability to be an effective leader. Leadership is not innate, nor is it taught. It is earned. It is every day, every interaction, every employee, every mistake, every success.

This book was created to pull back the curtain of effective leadership and to shine a light on the steps that you can take to become the leader that people choose to follow. This book will offer significant tools for you to utilize. You have to pick them up though. It is up to you to decide that you want to do the work. It is up to you to decide you want to earn the right to lead.

Manage
YOURSELF FIRST

I began my journey working at Walt Disney World as an intern in Disney's Animal Kingdom, in the land of Africa. On my very first day I walked in and an elderly gentleman came out, shook my hand and introduced himself as George. He proceeded to tell me that he was a retired vice president. He didn't need this job; he was just working to get park passes for his grandkids. He let me know that while he was there he was going to do an amazing job, but he wasn't going to show up early, work late and definitely would not come in on his days off. Finally, he said to me, "If this works for you then great. If not, you won't be here beyond six months," and he walked away.

This was my introduction into Disney leadership, and George was right—he was amazing while he was there. Another benefit of being a management intern at Walt Disney World is that I did everything that a true leader does. I had cast members that reported to me, I ran shift solo, I made decisions, I participated in disciplinary conversations. This was a crash course in leadership.

After being there for about two months, Disney did a little shuffle. They do this every year and a half to two years, shaking things up to keep it fresh and exciting. Normally one or two people get shifted to a different location, but this was a huge switch in leadership. By the time they were done moving leaders around, I was the most senior leader in my location. I'd only been there for two months. To say that there was a lot of stress and pressure, for both myself and the cast members, was an understatement.

One day I showed up early, super pixie dusted and excited, to open the land. I gathered all of the cast members to have our morning meeting, where I asked them to do something different. I don't even remember what it was, probably some minor shift that wasn't going to be a permanent change. I just wanted them to try it, and let me know how it went at the end of their shift. As I told them this, I saw George in the background. His body language was getting tense. Eventually, he stood up, took the notebook in his hand and slammed it down on a chair. He got up in my face and said, "I don't have to listen to you, you're just an intern. You mean nothing." It suddenly felt like the world had gotten way too small and I couldn't breathe. The loudest thing that I heard was silence.

All of these cast members were looking at me with their mouths open, waiting for me to respond. I know I'm supposed to tell you that in that moment I had the best answer. Instead, there were two voices battling for control in my head. The first was the voice of my leadership professors: a leader demands respect, a leader doesn't allow insubordination, a leader knows what to do.

The second was the voice of my mom. You see, I grew up in the Deep South where there were certain tenets that everybody knew instinctively upon birth. Tenet number one is to be polite. Tenet number two: bless your heart is not a compliment. Tenet number three: respect your elders.

So I did the only thing that I could think of. I told all the cast members, "It's okay, everybody go out to your stations. I'll come check on you all in a little while." And as the cast members went left into the theme park, I went right. Because to the right was a door outside into the cast break area, and I knew it would be empty because everybody was getting the park ready. As I was walking down the hall I felt a cast member tap me on the shoulder.

When I turned to look he said, "You didn't deserve that."

Feeling the tears well up in my throat, I said, "It's okay, just go out to your station, I'll be out in a little while." I walked a little bit faster until I finally reached the break area. I put my hand on the doorknob, opened the door and felt the warmth of the sun on my face. I cried, and it wasn't cute, princess-like tears. It was an ugly sob from my toes, and all I could think of at that moment was, "*I want to go home.*" But I knew this was one of the moments that determined whether or not I wanted to be a leader as much as I thought I did. So, I got up, went back through the door into the theme park, washed my face off in the bathroom, and then started checking in on my cast members, just as I said I would. Every time I went up to a cast member and saw that look of pity on their face, I kept moving forward.

George was the last cast member that I had to check on. As I came around the corner, I saw George, and George saw me. He started walking up to me with purpose. Y'all... I tensed up. Not a slight tense up, but a full body tense up. He may have surprised me once, but he wasn't going to surprise me twice. Before I could say anything, he said, "I'm so sorry."

Okay, didn't see that coming. Then he proceeded to share that when he left his big corporate job, he promised his wife that they would have balance. Because of all of the new changes in leadership, he was worried that the new leaders weren't going to respect the previous agreements, and that he would have to choose between his wife and his job. He knew without a doubt he would choose his wife. But he loved his job, he didn't want to have to give it up. And in that moment we met human-to-human, not leader to employee, not intern to cast member.

George taught me so much in that moment about what it means to be a good leader, and what it means to manage yourself first. If I would have jumped back at him the way that he jumped at me, we wouldn't have had that moment to understand and learn from each other. That relationship would have probably been destroyed. It also told me that as leaders, sometimes we're going to take the brunt of our employees' bad days, and if we are also having a bad day, it is significantly harder to do that. As you look into these next chapters to learn about what it means to manage yourself first, remember that you're not always going to have all of the answers, and that's okay.

CHAPTER 1

UNLEASHING THE POWER OF EMOTIONAL INTELLIGENCE

The Power of Emotional Intelligence

Have you ever had one of those pivotal moments, one that you may not realize is big at the time, but will forever influence your thinking moving forward? One of those moments happened when I was going to school for my MBA. I was doing a leadership intensive with one of my favorite professors, Dr. Bach. Now, Dr. Bach isn't much more than five feet tall, but she is fierce! She never let you get away with bullshit. So when she said something, I listened. There were about twenty of us in class and we were talking about emotional intelligence. I remember being very confused because I knew I was extremely self aware and had high emotional intelligence (EQ) regarding what was happening in my head, but other people's... y'all,

I was clueless. So I raised my hand and asked Dr. Bach if you could have high EQ in self and low EQ in others. She smiled her knowing-smile, and said, "Yes, you can." She then followed it up with something that I want you to pay very close attention to.

"EQ is not something that is fixed from birth, like IQ. EQ is more like a muscle. You can get better at it if you are willing to put in the work."[1]

Frankly, I was tired of not understanding people and constantly getting into trouble based on something that I said or did that someone else found upsetting. That became the day I vowed to raise my EQ. You, my dear reader, are going to get the crash course in EQ. But there's one thing I want you to take away from this if you take nothing else:

EQ is not an innate skill. You are not born with it. It is something that you can get better at. You just have to put in the work.

How does our brain process emotions? You may have heard something like, we have a thinking brain and an emotional brain, or a lizard brain. While this is an easy to understand concept, it doesn't tell the complete story. I had the pleasure of speaking with Dr. Rebekka Matheson[2], a professor of cognitive and behavioral neuroscience at Brigham Young University, and asked her to complete the story. She explained the ways in which science has shown our brain to work by giving an example of a water bottle.

> "Say there's a person and they're looking at a water bottle, and they decide to pick up that water bottle, and then they do it. There's three

steps. And one step is to get information about the water bottle—sensation. The last step is to pick up the water bottle— movement. And then in between, there is uniting the information about the water bottle to what you need, what it can do for you. What are your expectations? What will happen when you pick that thing up? How do you pick it up? What muscles do you use? And that's the intermediate step. So first you sense, then you process and interpret, and then you execute a response."

Emotional intelligence is what happens in the space between thinking about picking up the water bottle, and actually picking it up. But many times, especially in charged situations (like if the water bottle could yell at us in a meeting) the first step of thinking about doing something, happens automatically and without a directive. When that happens, if we are not prepared for it, the thinking and processing step can also happen extraordinarily quickly and without direction.

NYU psychologist Jonathan Haidt[3] uses an analogy that I have found useful. He says that the emotional responses in our brain are like an elephant and rider, where the rider represents our rational responses. If the elephant decides it *really* wants to go left, there is very little the rider can do other than hold on. This is how our brain works as well. Once our emotions get high, it is harder to think rationally and the rider of the elephant is simply along for the ride. That is why you may find yourself thinking it is a really good idea to pop off to your boss after you receive a negative review, but later regret it. The elephant wants to pop off. The rider knows better.

So the question becomes, how do we keep the rider in control of the elephant? Let's discuss the elephant for just a moment longer. An elephant doesn't fear many things[4]. In fact, one of the few things that an elephant fears is bees. You may be asking, "Why on earth are we talking about bees?" Well, imagine that you are the rider and want to make rational decisions, but your elephant is prone to make emotional decisions. You hear the buzzing of bees, and know that they will trigger your elephant to run off, and the only thing you will be able to do is hold on for dear life. So you decide to guide your elephant away from the trigger into safer territory.

That is the goal with Emotional Intelligence. It is not that we are trying to remove your triggers. We can't, we will always have them. Instead of removing them, the goal is to become aware of triggers so you can navigate the terrain and keep the rider in control instead of the elephant.

Loretta Ross, human rights activist, says, "I think we overuse that word 'trigger' when really we mean discomfort."[5] A trigger is something that causes our brain to remember past, painful experiences around traumatic events, and can cause certain symptoms from that experience to arise. When someone is triggered, it may seem small to observers, but the trigger can create a heightened level of anxiety, panic, anger or other intense emotions. Being uncomfortable, on the other hand, is a general emotional response to situations or experiences that challenge our comfort zones, beliefs, or values. We use the word a lot and in so doing, devalue the true experience of being triggered. When you ask yourself what triggers you, the answer isn't going to be things that cause minor discomfort, like someone chewing with their mouth open or smacking bubble gum. These are going to be moments that impact you in such a way that the elephant is in full control, and you are responding in a way that does not align with who you are or your values. Being triggered puts your body in defense mode. It is so important to understand your triggers, so you can respond the way you choose, not the way that your triggers dictate.

This would have been helpful information to know in the fall of 2013. My career at Walt Disney World was going swimmingly. I felt on top of the world and completely invincible, which is why I took a position that was definitely a stretch. No risk, no reward! I accepted a position as the third shift leader working at the World of Disney, which at the time, was the largest Disney store in the world. Every night, my small and mighty team would figure out a plan to put the entire building back together before the doors opened the next day. Up until that point in time, I had the privilege of working with, and for, leaders that believed in and trusted me. They would guide me and offer assistance as needed, but they didn't hover. Looking back, I think my leader at the time would have done the same if he had been given the opportunity, but we were both about to get caught up in a shitstorm the size of which I had never seen. And if I am being honest, it was a storm of my making.

There was a cast member who worked on the team I was leading. We will call her Alicia. Alicia was a challenge. It should have been no big deal, I have worked successfully with challenging employees before. In fact, it was kind of my speciality. But this time was different. Alicia wasn't just a challenge, she was a straight-up bully. And she had the ear of an executive. Early in my journey with this team, when we were still trying to figure things out, Alicia went to the executive and shared her perspective of what I was doing. A direct quote from her was that, "She hovers over me so close I can smell her deodorant." Anyone who knows me, knows I have space issues and I don't like people any closer than they need to be. To put it mildly, her perspective was not the entire truth. Without my side being asked, everything immediately shifted. I had a lot of attention on my team. I was told to stop picking on Alicia, as she became "off limits." What do you do when you have an employee that you can't lead and there are no other leaders on the shift? If you are me, you get mad.

Well, Alicia quickly figured out she could get away with whatever she wanted, and did as such. The other cast members saw me holding them accountable and saw her getting away with whatever she wanted. Even worse, they would have to pick up her slack. It was infuriating and I felt helpless. My leader was trying to manage the fallout and I was fighting against it because it wasn't fair (I know, life isn't fair). I assumed that because I was doing the right thing, it would all work out. I did not know that I was being triggered in multiple ways. The first is with bullying. My high school years were brutal. I was the target of loud, constant bullying, and it was one of the most helpless times in my life. So when I experienced that feeling of helplessness again, I doubled down. I also had a trigger about not being believed, or being ignored when I was saying that something was wrong. These came from childhood instances when I would share something that was happening, and I wasn't believed. Not only was that maddening, but I would be punished for lying, which caused a lot of helplessness and feelings of being out of control of my circumstances. I did not know about either of these triggers. In fact, I thought I was always in control.

The idea of being triggered wasn't mainstream at the time, so I didn't have anything to look at or consider. I was completely in responsive mode, full on defensive. My defensive mode is definitely to fight. It didn't go well. The situation was not resolved and the only thing I was successful at was to ruin my forward trajectory at Walt Disney World. It was a painful, painful experience. But there was also a lot of light in that experience that I wouldn't see until much later. You see, I was going to school for my MBA, with the aforementioned Dr. Bach, and she was able to help me think through my time at Disney. I learned more in those months about leadership, emotional intelligence, and myself than I have in the entirety of my leadership career. But, not a path I would recommend. To avoid being caught up in a shitstorm of your making, here are some questions I want you to spend some time with.

- What are your triggers?
- What causes you to react in a way counterintuitive to your beliefs about yourself, and your values?
- How do you react physically when you are triggered? For example, my belly gets really hot. When I start feeling heat in my belly, that is my first clue that my rider is losing control of my elephant.

As a leader, your bad days not only impact you, but also those around you. Your decisions can carry lifetime effects for other people, so you want to ensure that you are being intentional and showing up in the way you choose to, instead of in the way that your environment is dictating.

How do our brains process emotions?

The brain is a complex computer system. Old research theorized that the brain was broken up into three main systems, also known as a triune brain. We now know[6] it isn't as easy or neat as that, although it would have been fantastic if it was! I am going to oversimplify the way the brain works, but the goal is to give you an understanding of what happens when we react to stressors.

When a stimulus hits your brain, your brain processes this information to determine how you feel about it. Is this a threat? Are you happy? Should you be running? Let's say your brain determines that there is a threat. Our brains aren't very good at determining if the threat is a big threat, a physical threat, or a small threat. It just says threat. And our body reacts. When you feel threatened, your nervous system responds by releasing a flood of stress hormones, including adrenaline and cortisol, which rouse the body for emergency action. Your heart pounds faster, your muscles tighten, your blood pressure rises, your breath quickens, and your senses become sharper.[7]

One thing that needs to be pointed out is that nowhere on this list does it say you become smarter. In fact, studies have shown that we become dumber when we are threatened.[8] That is because so much of our resources are being pumped into the threat that the logical part of our brain (the rider) is no longer in control.

Why does this matter for you as a leader? Have you ever given difficult feedback to an employee and had them react strongly? Maybe they started crying, they got defensive, they just shut down, or my favorite—they started blaming everyone else? What do you do? Here is a hint—your brain will perceive their behavior as a threat. You will start getting wrapped up into your emotions. You may start thinking to yourself, "Oh god, are they mad at me? Do they not like me? I didn't mean to hurt their feelings. I am such an awful person."

You go down that rabbit hole and all of a sudden, you start telling them everything they have ever done right and how amazing they are OR you get angry and double down on the feedback and it comes out harsher than you intended. Your brain does not differentiate between a tiger attacking you, and you giving that person feedback. It is going to react the same way. Knowing that this is going to happen is your superpower. Knowing what you are likely to do is critical in these situations.

Have you heard of fight, flight, freeze, or please? We all have instincts in us to go into one of these 4 areas.

Fight

This is a response where the person gets ready to fight back. The fighting back could be verbal or physical. When a person with a "fight" reflex gets put under significant pressure, they will lash out. This makes sense when, for example, you were attacked by an animal while walking in the woods. In today's professional world, physical aggression isn't commonplace. But verbal aggression can show up much more often in the form of blaming, criticism, judging, snarky comments, and bullying.

Flight

The "flight" response occurs when someone is under significant pressure and runs. A time when this response would make sense is if you wake up and smell smoke. It is time to get away from the danger and out of the house. In the workplace, this would show up as walking away from confrontation, having a strong urge to leave a situation, or restless and fidgety legs and hands.

Freeze

The "freeze" response shows up as someone who appears to stop engaging. This may appear in someone who gets severe stage fright when delivering a presentation, stops talking and then just walks away. "Freeze" happens when we are so overloaded that we are hyper aware of everything around us, but we can't respond or, many times, move.

Please

"Please," also referred to as "Fawn," is a response that shows up when someone has tried" fight or flight," either currently or during a traumatic time in their past, and it did not work. "Please" manifests as excessive people-pleasing, even to the detriment of the individual. The person has a hard time saying no or setting boundaries, and will avoid conflict at all costs.

What is Emotional Intelligence?

So now we know we can learn EQ, and we have seen the multiple ways that we can show up during stress, but what exactly is EQ?

The term "Emotional Intelligence" was coined by Peter Salavoy and John Mayer in their article "Emotional Intelligence" in the journal, *Imagination, Cognition and Personality,* in 1990.[9] It became a more common phrase when it was made popular in the book, *Emotional Intelligence,* written by Dan Goleman in 1995. The term Emotional Intelligence, or EQ, was a direct play against the term IQ, or Intelligence Quotient, but they are very different. The definition of EQ is *"the ability to understand and manage your own emotions and feelings, as well those of others."* It seems easy enough when you see it written out as a definition, but the practice of EQ can be significantly harder. And the hardest part is we don't always have an accurate understanding of our own ability to be emotionally intelligent. So let's break it down even further.

In Goleman's work, he broke down Emotional Intelligence into 5 categories.

- Emotional self-awareness: knowing what one is feeling at any given time and understanding the impact those moods have on others
- Self-regulation: controlling or redirecting one's emotions; anticipating consequences before acting on impulse
- Motivation: utilizing emotional factors to achieve goals, enjoying the learning process and persevering in the face of obstacles
- Empathy: sensing the emotions of others
- Social skills: managing relationships, inspiring others and inducing desired responses from them

Let's look at each of these in the model that Goleman uses. You can see in the following table that the way we perceive and interact with emotional intelligence is broken into quadrants. On the y axis, we have recognition and regulation, on the x axis, we have self and social. What this means is that the self is what is happening with you, and social is what happens with others. Regulation is what is happening on the inside (what others cannot see) and recognition is the verbal and physical cues that others can see and experience. Spend some time with this and answer the following questions:

- What quadrant am I the strongest at? Why and how does it show up?
- What quadrant do I need to work on? What, if any, negative effects are happening because I am not as strong as I would like in this area?
- Would those closest to me, friends, family, mentor, agree about my strongest and weakest quadrants?

The thing about emotional intelligence, and why it is the very first concept we dig into, is that you cannot be an effective leader without first learning about your own emotional intelligence. You cannot effectively lead with, and through others, if you can't first lead yourself. Spend some time in this chapter and really think about where you are and where you want to be when interacting with any human, not just your employees. You cannot change anyone else, you can only change how you engage with them. As Jack Confield states, "You can't change anyone else, but people do change in relationship to your change. All relationships are a system, and when any one part of a system changes, it affects the other parts."[11]

Be the change—it will do you a world of good.

CHAPTER 2

CHECK YOURSELF BEFORE YOU WRECK YOURSELF

The butterfly effect[1] was explained to me that a butterfly will flap its wings in India and the change in air pressure will build and build and build and by the time it's done it causes a tornado in the United States somewhere. In short, small changes can create massive impacts. What I suggest is that the butterfly effect is something that we create as leaders. When we think about all of the things that leaders do, and all of the impacts that leaders have, sometimes knowingly and sometimes unknowingly, then we can see how these small changes can create these large impacts.

As a leader, have you ever introduced a new policy that you thought wasn't a big deal, and then all of a sudden it escalates into something more? And by the end of the day you have employees frantically coming to you, asking, "What is going on with this?"

That is an example of the butterfly effect. We can't predict every outcome to every decision that we make. But we can be intentional about the decisions that we make, why we make them, how we communicate them, and what we do.

There are a couple of ways to do this. I don't know about you, but I know that I tend to struggle when it comes to employees' strong emotions, no matter what that emotion is. So these are a couple of tools and tricks that have worked for me in the past.

Let them "feel their feels."

This one always brings me back to watching new leaders give their employees difficult feedback. The leader will think through all of the ways the conversation could go horribly wrong. They spend so much time thinking of all the ways it will be awful that they forget to spend any time preparing for the conversation. Then, when the employee reacts in a strong way, the leader is stumped on what to do next and gets in their head. To clarify, when I say a strong way, I mean the employee is not necessarily doing anything they shouldn't do. They are being professional, but maybe they are crossing their arms and leaning back, speaking loudly, or in an angry voice, or even worse... the dreaded tears appear.

Either way there are strong emotions involved, and you can watch the leader physically recoil from this situation. Afterwards in conversations, many times the leader may comment on how unprofessional that employee was, or how disrespectful that employee was. The response to that leader tends to always be, "Do you like being told that you suck at something?" And the leader looks confused and offended and says, "Well, no!"

So, if we don't like to be told that we suck at something, why do we hold people accountable to such high degrees of professionalism? We're doing it professionally. We're doing it respectfully. We're doing it with compassion and empathy. But when it comes down to it we are telling them that they are not performing at a level that we need them to perform and then we get upset when they show emotions. I'd be more upset if I was talking to an employee telling them that they need to improve at something and they showed no emotions.

One of my colleagues, Katie Fling[2], made an observation regarding how we handle others' emotions:

"In order for us to be comfortable with other's emotions, we have to be comfortable with those same emotions within ourselves."

Think about it, if a person was never given permission to cry, or they were taught that tears are weak, then how will they have the tools to be able to handle another person's tears? This is only one reason why we may be uncomfortable with strong emotions in other people, but it is a reason to explore. We need to allow room for employees to "feel their feels". When you are giving feedback, it has nothing to do with you. You are doing it for the employee.

This was a lesson that one of my favorite leaders, Michele, taught me. I was working at Disney's Blizzard Beach and I had been given an amazing opportunity. I was asked to be a temporary leader. When asked, I had been making $7 an hour working in a sports store. When I accepted, I was a salary leader. It was only temporary but it was a chance to prove myself and get a coveted permanent leadership position. All I knew was at the end of the four months I would be going back to that sports store, unless I was the most amazing leader ever.

The thing that you need to know about me is that I hate sports. Working at a sports store caused complications. The guests would come in and ask for, I don't know... Chicago Bulls merchandise. I would look at them, dead serious, and ask, "Is that football, basketball?" They would be offended and I would get yelled at. That was my day. So when I tell you that I did not want to go back to the sports store I cannot express just how much I did not want to go back.

I was going to be so amazing that they couldn't even imagine sending me back to the sports store. That was the plan anyway. But, it wasn't working. The thing is, even to this day, I cannot tell you why it wasn't working. Now, for those of you who know me, you know that I have a little bit of an intense personality. That intensity has diminished as I have gotten older and hopefully a little bit wiser.

At the beginning of my career with Disney, I was at my most intense in my entire life, so I can imagine that Michele was a little nervous about telling me I wasn't doing as well as she had hoped. The day had finally come. I knew I was struggling, I knew I wasn't doing a good job. I could not figure out why, and I was beyond frustrated. If I'm being honest, I was probably a little manic. Michele grabs me from the floor and brings me into her office and— I'll never forget— she looks at me with kindness and says, "I don't know what you're doing, but it doesn't appear to be working."

In that moment, instead of feeling frustration, I felt overwhelming gratitude that somebody had actually said it out loud. There is nothing worse than knowing that you are doing a bad job, but not knowing why, and being afraid to say anything because you're hoping that nobody else will have noticed. When Michele brought it up and put it out into the world for us to actually have a conversation about it, it felt like a weight had been lifted off my shoulders. In the next few hours we sat down and she taught me what it means to be a leader at Walt Disney World.

How many times do we expect employees or leaders to be fantastic from day one? We attract them to our organization because of how powerful our culture is, how amazing everything is, and how different we are from the competition, but then expect them to fit in immediately without helping them acclimate to this amazing and unique culture?

What Michele did, was teach me how to be a leader at Walt Disney World, not just a leader. She also gave me space to feel my feelings. There were a lot of feelings that day. There was frustration, there was disappointment in myself, and there were tears. Through every single emotion, Michele met me point-by-point to help me get over that hump. I had no doubt that she was fully in that moment and there for me. She wasn't giving me feedback because she was frustrated or angry. She was doing it because she believed I could do better and sincerely wanted to help me get there.

I will tell you that the worst day of my professional career came many years later. Michele was the first person that I went to, and as soon as she closed the door in her office, I broke down to a level that I have not since done. My heart was broken and my soul was hurting. I went to her because I knew that she would give me the space to "feel my feels," and she did it that day the same way that she always had. There's trust built in these moments, when you allow the humans that work for you to be fully human.

As leaders, we can fall into the trap of only wanting the good parts of our employees. We only want the positive, the happy, the productive. We get uncomfortable when there are emotions that are shown that we don't consider positive.

Give your employees a safe space to "feel their feels". Set boundaries for what is, and is not acceptable. Some of the ways that leaders have found that are helpful, is to let their employees know that they are allowed to feel these uncomfortable and intense emotions, and leaders will be there for them when this happens. What they do expect is that the situation will never turn personal, meaning that the employee is allowed to feel disappointed, frustrated or angry at the situation. These are the times when checking yourself is one of the most important things to do, because when you are in these situations and emotions are high, you must make the space for your employee. Remember, it has nothing to do with you.

The Power of Silence.

When we are giving feedback, or are in uncomfortable situations, we sometimes end up talking in circles. We may ask a question, talk through it, and then ask it again. This may leave an employee confused, so we talk again when there is uncomfortable silence.

We are not giving our employees the space that they need to consider what the question was, and what's happening. Another consequence is that we are giving them a reason to not have to talk, even when it is a situation where we really need their input. So we have a superpower as leaders called *silence,* and we don't use this superpower nearly enough. In fact, many times we treat this superpower as kryptonite and completely disregard and talk over the silence that we need in a given situation. We do this because it makes us feel better, but again, when we are having conversations where we should be considering emotional intelligence and managing ourselves first, it is important to understand that it is not about us. When we are giving employees the space that they need to process and have these conversations, we need to understand to also give them silence.

Now the hard thing about silence is actually being quiet, the easy thing about silence is we have ways to practice this skill throughout the day. We don't need this skill only in these important meetings. We can practice it with our loved ones, other types of meetings, at work, or in conversations with our friends. And there's a magical thing that happens when we leave space for silence. We learn incredible things about other people.

My husband, Miles, is my absolute rock. I adore him more than I can tell you, and if I am being 100 percent honest with you (which I always try to be 100 percent honest with you), one of the reasons why I love and married this man is because he doesn't talk that much. Because as you have probably discovered through my chosen career of professional speaking, I do like to talk. This became a problem when we were having challenging conversations.

He wouldn't respond and I would think that he wasn't as invested as I was.

I was talking to one of my leaders, Diane, and I was fussing about something. She looked at me with a smirk, a kind smirk, but a smirk, and asked if I had stopped talking long enough for him to respond. I thought about it for a moment, and chose not to answer that question. When I went home later that evening, we sat down to continue the conversation, and after I made a comment that was intense for both of us, I was intentionally quiet. I gave Miles the space that he needed to be able to respond. And he did! What I learned in that moment is that Miles is a processor. He needs time to think through what we are talking about, and choose his words before he responds. By always talking over the silence, I was never giving him that time. So this became a new aspect in our relationship. We created the space he needed to think through what I had said, and what he wanted to say by being silent. So believe me when I say that there are so many opportunities in our day to actually think through and offer silence.

Start taking advantage of those moments. Treat it like a muscle that you're trying to train. Because the other really incredible thing about silence, is that it allows us to determine how we want to show up.

Managing ourselves first isn't found in talking, it is found in the moments of silence. It happens when we have the ability to think through and choose how we want to show up, instead of just reacting to a situation. Use your superpower of silence.

You will not always have the answer.

This is a hard one for many of us.

As leaders, we get paid to have the answers. We get paid to look into our crystal ball, predict the future, understand how things are going to work, and make just the right decision to be able to lean forward. We get penalized if we are not making the correct decisions. I think as a society we are getting better at allowing people the space to mess up, so that they understand what it feels like and what to do differently next time—but it is still not a happy situation. And so when we find ourselves in a situation where we're not sure what to do, we put on our armor. We shut down or react instead of being intentional. This can be one of the quickest ways that we wreck ourselves. This can be where the butterfly has unintended effects that go for miles, and completely decimate the emotional currency that we have built with our teams.

There is great power in silence, and there is also great power in saying, "I don't know." That was one of the things that Disney taught us when we were thinking about guest service. If we did not know the answer when somebody asked, we would say, "I don't know" or, "That's a great question, let me find out the answer for you." We would then make sure that we had contact information so that we could follow up with them. We would give them a timeline as to when we would be following up. We would create this emotional comfort for the guests that showed them we had their back and would take care of their concerns.

But then as leaders, we were expected to have the answers for our cast members. Many of us wondered what would happen if we could use the same "I don't know" tactic with them. Would that have the same positive effect? Would it build emotional trust and make them feel like they were being taken care of? And so we leaned into that. We started telling our cast members, "You know what, that's a great question. I'm not sure, give me 24 hours to find out."

Another lesson around communicating with your employees was a lesson learned when I was pregnant. Forgetting items was a real problem during pregnancy (#pregnancybrainis-real). I didn't want to risk forgetting about something that was important to my cast, so I started letting them know, and giving them permission that if I have not responded to their question within a specific time frame, they should follow up.

I was blunt with them. "Y'all, my brain is not working the way that I need it to work. This is important to you and it's important to me, but there's a high probability that if I am not able to start working on this by the time I get to my office, I'm going to forget." This did two things. The first was that it gave them permission to follow up with me. The second was that I was role modeling what it meant to be imperfect in the workplace. It showed them that it was okay to set boundaries for mutual success. At no point did a cast member roll their eyes or get upset when I told them this. They all said okay, and felt more comfortable following up with me if they did not hear within the specified time frame. Not having the answer does not make you weak, nor does it make you a bad leader. It does not mean that you are not doing your job. It means that you are human and you do not know everything. Accepting that is a sign of authenticity and strong leadership.

Think about it– if somebody comes up to you and asks you a question in an area of your expertise, and you get to geek out on all this information that you have worked so hard for, how does that make you feel? In most cases assuming the person asking isn't somebody that you despise, you're probably going to feel pretty good about that. So why wouldn't we give our employees the opportunity to feel good and explain something to us? When we think about checking ourselves before wrecking ourselves, and the fact that we are the butterfly, we recognize that we have these unintended consequences. The ability to say 'I don't know' and then work on finding out the answer is critical to tying all of this together.

So the thing to remember is that we need to allow our employees the space to "feel their feels", give them the space to lean into whatever emotion that they are having at that given time, lean into our superpower of silence, and finally, accept that we don't have to have all of the answers.

My favorite quote in this regard is by holocaust survivor and author of *Man's Search for Meaning*[3], Viktor Frankl. He states, "Between stimulus and response there is a space. In that space is our power to choose our response. In our response lies our growth and our freedom."

That space is where we manage ourselves first. Take advantage of the space. Choose who you want to be and how you want to show up instead of just reacting.

Tina James[4], Retired Chief People Officer of H-E-B, states that to truly avoid wrecking yourself, you also need to surround yourself with a "2 AM Club". The 2 AM Club is a small group of individuals that will do two things.

1. They will support you.
2. They will tell you the truth.

It is really important that they are willing to do both of these things. My husband, Miles, thinks I hang the moon. He loves me completely and unconditionally. I love this about him, but we also both realize that he will not always see when I am doing something that probably isn't the best choice. When he does see this, he will absolutely tell me, but it doesn't happen often. He gives me unlimited support, but he doesn't think I screw up that much.

On the other hand, I have had people in my life that will gleefully tell me when I am screwing up, but there is no support. They are doing it simply to bring themselves joy. If these people are telling me I am screwing up, I tend not to listen with both my head and heart.

There are a few people, less than a handful, that fit both of these categories. These are the individuals that I can call at 2 AM and work through the really hard things. These are the things that may or may not be my fault, the things that I am too close to and having a hard time seeing the other side. I know these individuals will both support me, and tell me the honest and kind truth. Your 2 AM club is made up of the individuals that help to keep you from wrecking yourself. They are the ones that will tell you when you are not showing up as the best version of yourself.

CHAPTER 3

STRIKING THE BALANCE - THE FINE LINE OF AUTHENTICITY

When we think about authentic leadership, a lot of times, people imagine we're going to be sitting around in a circle and sharing our deepest and darkest secrets. This is not the case.

As leaders, we walk a fine line of being authentic but not too authentic. There is such a thing as too much authenticity. We have probably seen and felt it from others. Authentic leadership is knowing who you are and knowing how you want to show up, then consistently showing up that way. Knowing your strengths, your opportunities, what you know, what you don't know and your opinions versus your facts all create leadership. So if you were thinking to yourself that you are going to have to cry, this is not that chapter. Instead, we are going to look at what authentic leadership is, how it shows up in the workplace, and what it means when you are told that you need to be authentic.

According to the Center for Creative Leadership, authentic leaders are those who are true to themselves and the principles that guide them.[1] The Center for Creative Leadership continues to say that, "Although these leaders may be in charge, their principles ultimately govern them, and people ultimately matter."

So when we think about authentic leadership, there is no hard definition for what this is. There is no black-and-white answer. Authentic leadership is going to depend on who you are, what your values are, the organization that you work for and the pressures that influence the person that you are today. If you're looking for a quick and easy answer, there isn't one. So let's look at what we need to do to consider authentic leadership.

One of the first things that we need to do when considering authentic leadership, is to rethink what leadership means. If you consider shows like *Mad Men*, it has a very antiquated style of what leadership looks like. But for many of us, before we get into the workplace, this is what we have seen presented as leadership and maybe what we have experienced in our summer jobs. So it makes sense that once we get into the workplace, we are a little bit confused as to what to do. College and leadership courses often make leadership sound like a "one size fits all" practice. We know this isn't true, so what is effective leadership?

A great example of this comes from 19 year old Snoopslimes CEO, Jungmin Kang.[2] Jungmin started her slime business when she was 13 years old by borrowing $200 from her parents. In the six years since the business started, it has grown to over $11 million in annual revenue, 40 employees, and millions of social media followers. Jungmin was just named to the Forbes 30 Under 30 List and continues to influence an entire industry. My daughter and I found Snoopslimes via TikTok and fell in love with the product and the culture. So you can imagine how thrilled I was when Jungmin agreed to be interviewed for this book.

Her family moved to the United States from Korea when she was six. She didn't speak English and it was a bit of a culture shock. Her Korean culture is extremely important to her, and part of the Snoopslime brand is that they use slime to imitate food. It is one of Jungmin's super powers actually. She can take almost anything edible and recreate it in slime.

She found herself hesitating when it came to sharing her Korean culture with her followers and customers though. She wanted to share this piece of herself and her company, but wasn't sure how to do it. Enter *Squid Games*. When the Netflix show went viral, Jungmin found her chance. She introduced a slime based on the candy "dalgona."

The slime was received extremely well and Jungmin realized that her followers were hungry (pun intended) for her to share this more authentic side of herself. She also realized that she had an opportunity to influence a new generation of consumers into different cultures, different foods, and different experiences.

Cultural exploration and curiosity continue to be a hallmark of Snoopslimes, not only with Jungmin, but with those that choose to work for Snoopslimes.

Jungmin's advice when considering your uniqueness and authenticity and whether or not to share: "Embrace it. That is the culture you want to build for your team, so embrace it and share first."

Many times, we know effective and authentic leadership as soon as we see it. We definitely know when it is lacking. But when we see it, sometimes we *don't* think about it.

You know effective leadership when things are going well. And if you have things that are going well, chances are, your leader is authentic. They have surrounded themselves with someone who balances their opportunities. They know their strength, lean in when they should, and back out when they shouldn't be involved. So it's really hard to describe authentic leadership when considering this, because we take it for granted. We just assume that that is the way that things should be. But then when we find ourselves in a position of leadership, and have to figure out what authentic leadership is and how to do it, we realize how hard it actually is. But because we have taken it for granted in the past, it's hard to pull up examples of what it looks like. Or, if you have a specific example in mind, it may not fit your leadership style.

When I first started working at Walt Disney World, I made sure to surround myself with mentors that could help me in areas of weakness. The people that I admire the most (many of whom I have mentioned already) are the ones that I tried very hard to emulate. But it wasn't working, because I am not them. Yes, I could appreciate the areas of strength that they had that were my areas of opportunity, and I could work to improve those areas. But I couldn't be that person. And every time I tried, it would come across as unauthentic or insincere. When I would read or hear about authentic leadership, the frustration would continue because I was being me, but every time I was me, I was told to tone it down. Many years later, I came across an explanation of authenticity[3] that resonated with me and truly helped me understand.

Take a moment and think through what color you feel represents you. If that is too nebulous for you, choose your favorite color.

Got it?

Now, pick a shade of that color that represents you. For example, my color would be purple and my shade would be a deep, rich, royal purple. No violet anywhere in sight.

Imagine your most authentic self lies within that shade, but the color itself represents you. Sometimes, when around different people or environments, you may need to adjust the shade. For example, sometimes, I may need to be violet. It doesn't mean I am going against my core self. I am not violating my values, I am not trying to be someone else. I am simply adjusting my shade to the environment.

This is what it means to be authentic in different environments. I will always be me. I will always be purple. But sometimes I may need to be burgundy or violet instead of royal purple.

A quick note: authenticity also isn't a weapon. It drives me bonkers when someone gets called out for bad behavior and their response is, "I was just being authentic." Or, "You want me to be honest don't you?" When someone uses authenticity or honesty as a shield, it is just an excuse for bad behavior.

How to be as authentic as possible.

Now that we know that there is no one-size-fits-all leader, we need to rethink leadership image. When you picture a successful leader, what comes to mind? Is it the teacher that you had when you were in third grade, or is it the very first leader that you had out of college? When we think of the ideal leader, we need to understand what we're thinking about because when we think about ourselves in a leadership position, that is who we are comparing ourselves against. This is also the person that we may subconsciously be trying to emulate.

The other piece of being an authentic leader is exactly what we have been talking about–managing yourself first. Understanding how you show up in moments of strength, and how you show up when all hell is breaking loose, will help you identify where you currently are, and will allow you the information to begin identifying where you want to be.

If you can't predict how you are going to show up, then your team can't predict it either. One of the biggest pieces of authentic leadership is that you are consistently you, no matter the situation. If you don't know who that is, chances are your employees don't either. So, when things do hit the fan, they are not only having to deal with the fallout of whatever that looks like, but they are also having to predict how you are going to show up. Understanding how you react in moments of stress, your triggers, what brings you joy, what fills your bucket, what frustrates you, and what disappoints you, are all important in being an authentic leader.

Another piece of authentic leadership is understanding who you want to be when everything is falling apart. What I mean by this is, what are your values? What do you find important?

One of mine is that I live by individuality, meaning that no matter who you are, I'm going to do my best to create space at the table for you. This is really easy when I like the people that are coming to the table. It's really hard when I don't like the people that are coming to the table. It is important to keep in mind that if I value individuality, I have to accept people as they come. If I am going to stand up here and tell you that nobody is broken and we should stop trying to fix people, I also have to stop treating people as if they are broken and need to be fixed. It's a struggle, especially today when there's so many varying issues and so many areas that we feel super passionate about.

Another value that I have is safety. Meaning that if I am at the table, I am going to create a safe space for everybody there. These two values can cause conflict within me, because when there is someone alienating others or being cruel and abusive, I cannot balance individuality with safety. Knowing which value I prioritize—safety or individuality—will guide me on deciding how I show up in that instance. But if

I'm not very clear on what my values are, then it causes a lot of strife and conflict. This is why it is so important for you to spend time with yourself to understand your values and what is important to you.

If you're unsure where to get started, I highly recommend going to Brene' Brown's Dare to Lead hub.[4] There are a ton of resources, one of which involves identifying your top three values. When you can identify your top three values, you are significantly closer to understanding who you are as an authentic leader. Understanding your values helps you show up in the way that you want to show up when things aren't going well. It is easy to be an authentic leader when everything is going according to plan. Challenge comes when it is not.

Where are your blind spots?

The next step in authentic leadership is understanding where your blind spots are. What are some of the things that you like, what are some of the things that you don't like, and what are some of the things you can tolerate, but you'd be okay if they weren't there? This includes behaviors and people. Does someone loudly chewing gum drive you bonkers? Are you automatically drawn to someone who enjoys the same TV show you watch? Do you tend to be more drawn to charismatic individuals? Or do you find people that are extremely extroverted exhausting, and you tend to steer clear of them?

This concept is important because you are going to be responsible for leading others. If you are not sure what personality traits you steer clear of, you may make decisions that have nothing to do with the person, and more to do with how you feel about one of their personality traits. As leaders, we influence people's lives. We make decisions that influence their careers. We make decisions that can put them in a position or direction that maybe they don't want to go. So understanding how you show up, what is important to you, and what your likes and dislikes are critical in making effective decisions for the people that choose to follow you.

Another aspect of blind spots that can be uncomfortable to discuss, but is extremely relevant for leaders, is in diversity, equity, and inclusion. Knowing your blind spots and biases is critical. Early on in my consulting career, I was in a meeting with a group of leaders who were discussing an upcoming promotion. They were running through internal candidates that they wanted to consider for the position. They came across a female candidate who had recently had a child. When her name came up, one of the leaders in the room, with the best of intentions, asked if she should be on the list. "After all, she has a baby at home. Is now the best time to uproot her family?" Many of the leaders in the room got quiet and looked at each other uncomfortably. Someone eventually spoke up and pointed out a male candidate with a new baby had already been approved for the list. There was some discussion, the leader recognized their error and unconscious bias, and used it as a learning experience. Many times, when we consider Diversity, Equity, and Inclusion challenges, they aren't the in-your-face challenges, like overt racism or discrimination.

It happens in the smaller moments, the moments where the intention is positive, like in the previous example. We need to be on the lookout for when these moments creep in, and be ready to speak up. We also need to be aware of when we are likely to have these moments. The insidious thing about unconscious bias is that we are not aware of it until it begins causing problems for someone else, and it feels like it is easier to avoid it than confront it head on.

When I was going on my own journey to uncover the areas of bias I had, I became frustrated with myself. I was talking with my coach one day and shared with her that it felt like I wasn't making any progress. When I would run into a situation where I was aware of bias and trying to change it, I would still get thoughts that were not helpful and were a violation of my values and who I was trying to become. For example, if I was at the beach and saw a large woman wearing a bikini, my first thought was that maybe she should cover up. My second thought was a corrective thought, something along the lines of, "You know what, she can rock that bikini and kudos to her for being out here living her best life".

My coach said something powerful, "When that happens, your first thought is what you have been taught. Your second thought is who you are trying to be." This was life changing! As you are going along your journey, don't give power to your first thought. Give power to your second thought. Don't shy away from uncovering your areas of bias and be truly honest with yourself where you may have some work to do, but don't give up because it feels too hard. Everytime you introduce the second thought, you are making small steps that will add up to major change over time.

Authentic leadership simply means showing up as our true, authentic selves. Knowing who we are under pressure, who we are when things are going well, our shortcomings, and our strengths is key. You have heard me say this multiple times in this chapter, and that is because that is what authentic leadership is. So the next time you consider what an authentic leader looks like, realize that there is no one-size-fits-all. Are you authentically showing up in the way that feels right to you?

N ow that we know how to Manage Ourselves First, let's look at the power of purpose.

While I worked at Disney we knew our purpose—that we make magic.

Diane (my leader) came in one day and solidified our purpose in a unique way. Instead of, "we make magic," it became "we make magic, period". Not, "we make magic, question mark?" Are we going to make magic if it's convenient? Are we going to make magic if it's affordable? Are we going to make magic if we feel like it?

It became: *We make magic, period.* Every guest. Every time.

I decided to test this particular theory one day. A family of two children and a mother came in. The mom was doing that mom-smile thing that moms do when they're not super happy, but they're trying to fake it for their kids. The kids weren't even trying to pretend to be happy. I walked over, excited if I'm telling you the truth, because I had just gone through some customer service training. I was excited to put it to the test. So I leaned over and I asked mom in my most chipper of voices, how are you doing? And in a voice devoid of emotion, she said the infamous words that we all say when we're not feeling super well, "I'm fine."

Me: "You're in the happiest place on earth, you can't just be fine. What's going on? Tell me, I can help."
Her: "No, I don't want to bother you."
Me: "I have 4 hours left on my shift, bother away."

She took a big sigh and began to tell me her story.

A quick side note: have you ever asked a question and not been prepared for the answer? This was one of those times for me.

Her: "My husband died 6 months ago, and since he's died I haven't seen my kids smile. I really need to see my kids smile. I figured if anybody could do it, it would be Disney, because as you say, this is the happiest place on earth. But it's not working."

Me: In a quiet voice "Have you taken them to meet their favorite characters?"

Her: "Yes."

Me: "But what about their favorite attractions?"

Her: "Yes."

Me: "What about…"

Here she cut me off, and in a voice that was half desperation and half anger she loudly proclaimed, "We have done everything."

At that point I didn't know what to say or do but I knew if there was ever a family that needed magic, it was this family.

I asked what they were going to be doing next, and she said that they were going to Universal Studios. They loved Harry Potter. Their dad used to read them Harry Potter every night before they went to bed. I wished her a magical time and as I was walking away, I looked back and told her to stop by guest relations on her way into Universal.

Exasperated, she asked, "Why?"

I said, "It looks like your family could use a little bit of magic," and then I went to my office feeling the weight of this family.

I picked up the phone and gave Universal Studios a call. It is important to note that Disney and Universal are rivals, and we can be pretty competitive. So it is no shock that when I called and said that I was calling from Walt Disney World they immediately went to hang up. I stopped them and quickly explained the situation, and told them everything about this family. I asked if there was anything that they had that might help. They told me about the Harry Potter wands. You see, these are wands that interact with the park. It was brand new technology at the time and they *are* 100% magical. However, they are $50 per wand.

Why are theme parks so expensive?

I asked if they would consider paying for them and they quickly assured me that they would not. I realize that at Disney, our purpose is, "we make magic." Universal's purpose is adventure and excitement. These are two different purposes that show up in two different ways.

So I decided to purchase two.

Me: "I would like 2 please, what would the total be?"
Universal: "$113.82. How will you be paying?"
Me: "My Walt Disney World corporate card."
Universal: 😂😂😂😂😂😂😂
Me: .....

I waited a few moments while they finished laughing, and then we finished the transaction.

I realized at that moment that my job might be worth exactly $113.82.

But a few days later, when the family came back in, I knew it was absolutely worth it. The mom had a big smile, and the kids were acting like kids. The little boy rushes over to show me the letter that Harry Potter had left him, and the girl, not to be outdone, rushes over to show me the letter that Hermione Granger had left her. I see you Universal, you got some magic too.

And as the mom hugged her kids and looked at me with tears in her eyes, I absolutely knew that we had done the right thing. The next step was going to be convincing my boss that spending $113.82 at a competitor was the right thing. You'll hear about that a little bit later.

This story is one example of the power of having a purpose. This is not just a personal purpose, but a team purpose as well. A purpose allows your team to know what to do when you are not there to answer questions. Being able to articulate the purpose, and then aligning your employees to the purpose isn't easy, but it is well worth it. The next three chapters will begin uncovering the steps needed to be able to do these things.

CHAPTER 4

THE REAL PURPOSE OF PURPOSE

You have probably heard of the Glassdoor "Great Places to Work" lists that come out every year. Pre-2020, the top twenty or so of that list was pretty stable. Since 2020, it has been shaken up in a big way. If I asked you to name the top ten companies that were listed for 2023, who would you choose? Go ahead and take a moment and write them down. Ready?

Once you are done, head to the next page to see how many you got right.

The list for 2023 was:[1]

1. Gainsight
2. Box
3. Bain & Company
4. McKinsey & Company
5. NVIDIA
6. MathWorks
7. Boston Consulting Group
8. Google
9. ServiceNow
10. In-N-Out Burger

How many did you guess? Were you expecting to see Apple, Meta, Disney or similar companies on the list? They used to be there, consistently and without fail. So why has that changed? Why are there new companies heading to the top?

In short, it is about "purpose."

It is easy to say that a company has purpose during the easy times, but during the hard times, a company must *show* it has purpose, not just say it. But what is purpose? What is culture? Why are they so important?

Employee reviews of the top 10 are excellent, and all show purpose.

A Gainsight employee said, "Gainsight truly lives and breathes its company values and *tries winning in business while being human-first.*"

A Box employee reported, "Talented colleagues that reinforce a collaborative culture, making remote employees feel included."

An In-N-Out employee said, "The company will always take care of its associates, even through rough times economically."

You can see in these comments that the employees have strong feelings about what it means to be employed at these companies.

In 2020, Glassdoor COO said it well, "In addition to putting culture and mission at the core of how they operate, the winners stand out for promoting transparency with employees, offering career growth opportunities and providing work driven by impact and purpose."

Employees are demanding more from their organizations, and the organizations that get it are the ones that are thriving. The organizations that are living by old-school ideals are struggling.

Transparency, growth, impact all create "purpose."

Okay, so what is purpose?

The University of California Berkeley defines it as, "an abiding intention to achieve a long-term goal that is both personally meaningful and makes a positive mark on the world."[2]

This rings true for me.

Gone are the days when employees went to work simply for a paycheck. With vast amounts of knowledge and more resources than ever before, employees want to not only earn a living, but also to leave the world a little better than when they found it. It is also important to understand that purpose is not a one size fits all thing that a CEO creates and hands down. Purpose is truly personal. The company's purpose may be on their website, but the employees can tell you what the true purpose is. They know it because they can see it, feel it, and live in it.

Nancy Duarte, author, Ted Talk speaker,[3] and founder of *Duarte.com*, knows a thing or two about finding purpose. Before the internet, *Duarte* was a scrappy company offering corporate support services such as print work, graphic design, multimedia, and upgrading presentations. PowerPoint was on the scene and death by PowerPoint was a real thing. When the internet, and Silicon Valley, started booming, *Duarte* was booming right along with them. Then came the "Dot-com" crash. Nancy and her company were trying to figure out where they fit in this new world. Around this time, Jim Collins published his book *From Good to Great* and in it, he mentions the Hedgehog Concept based on the Greek parable about the Fox and the Hedgehog, "The fox knows many things, but the hedgehog knows one big thing."

The Hedgehog Concept is, "a simple, crystalline concept that flows from deep understanding about the intersection of three circles: 1) what you are deeply passionate about, 2) what you can be the best in the world at, and 3) what best drives your economic or resource engine."[4]

Nancy read this and understood that she needed to narrow her focus to the thing they are best at: presentation design.

In her words, "that was probably one of the biggest risks and counterintuitive moves I made in a crisis. I said, 'Okay, we're going to shutter the doors on everything except presentations.'" Duarte stopped doing multimedia print, packaging, and web and they doubled down on presentations. Nancy realized that presentation design was the thing that nobody had actually made great yet. They were the first ones to actually redefine what this medium was and what it could be.

At a time when *Duarte* was lost and trying to find its way, Nancy chose the company's true north, their purpose, and they have continued to lean into that ever since. That purpose has grown into a unique culture where lucky individuals can call themselves a "duartian," and know what it means to be a part of a team that has influenced some of the greatest presentations in the world.

This is the power of purpose.

It always infuriates me when a company says its purpose is something along the lines of, "To give our customers the best experience they have ever had," but when I try to return something, their policies make it damn near impossible. The employees bear the brunt of that frustration. They see the disconnect between the purpose advertised, and the purpose in the operation. This causes a lot of frustration on their part, and the part of the customer.

Another source of frustration with employees and their leaders is that it is all about the money. When I am coaching, training, or delivering keynote speeches to leaders, money will generally come up. An employee is unhappy that one of their peers is making more than them, they didn't get a bonus and are upset, or maybe they asked for a raise and were denied. All of these statements create negative responses from leaders such as, "Oh well, I don't set salaries, it's not my fault," and the leader is either frustrated, or wipes their hands of the issue. While money is important to employees, after a certain income level, it is no longer the motivating factor.

According to a 2023 Princeton and Wharton study, money buys happiness up to around $100,000 and after that, happiness still increases with more money, but not at such a drastic rate.[5] If money isn't the motivating influence, then why does an employee get angry if another employee is making more than them? Think back to when you had your 17th birthday. Think of a sibling or a cousin. Imagine that your grandparents got your sibling or cousin a brand new sports car convertible for their 17th birthday. When it was your turn, you got a beat up old clunker that leaked oil and squealed every time you turned the wheel to the left (yes, there is a specific car I am thinking of). How would that feel? You would probably be a little hurt, if not a lot.

Is it really about the cars though?

No, it is about being treated in a fair manner. We notice when things are unfair and as a species, we tend to focus on it. The same thing can be said about bonuses or rejected raises. It comes down to how the employee holds their worth versus how they perceive a company sees their worth. When there is a disconnect between these two areas, negative feelings are likely to occur. Salaries are a representation of how a company values their employees. It isn't always about the money, but more of a sense of value or a lack thereof.

In fact, according to the Harvard Business Review,[6] 90 percent of employees are willing to earn less to do more meaningful work. You have probably heard that statistic before. If we know that employees are willing to earn less to do more meaningful work, why do we keep making the same complaints about money? Because it is easy to blame everything on money. Money is black and white. You make enough, or you don't. Purpose is significantly harder, but so much more rewarding. 73 percent of employees who say they work at a "purpose driven" company are engaged, compared to just 23 percent of those who don't.[7] A strong sense of purpose is directly tied to a strong culture. It is clear that above all else, including pay, employees remain with companies when their ideals align with the company's purpose.

Tyrone Frost[7], a retired Air Force pilot, who now works for major airlines states that, "With any organization that's successful, and with any leadership that is promoting or providing information, there has to be a clear vision and goal, which then grabs and motivates people to be on their team."

H-E-B, a grocery retailer based in Texas, knows all about purpose and motivating people. Since their humble beginnings in 1905, this company has continued to focus on a, "people first" culture. This focus has consistently earned them top ranks in the great places to work list. Tina James, who retired at the end of 2022 as the Chief People Officer, explains more about the purpose. "There are a lot of companies who say they have a purpose. Saying that you have a purpose is easy. Consistently delivering on the purpose is the hard part. When hard decisions are made, and a company has to choose door number one, the easy door that doesn't align with purpose, or door number two, the hard door that is all about the purpose, does the company make the hard decision to live into their purpose or is it simply a motto on the wall and not lived out?"

Tina saw this play out first hand a few years after she joined the company. The Guadaluple river in South Texas had flooded. H-E-B rallied to take care of the impacted communities. Tina had a special job, which was to assist her employees, also known as partners. Tina sat in a breakroom in multiple stores with pen and paper with a line of Partners to speak to.

She asked questions like, "What did you lose? What do you need? How can we help you?"

She wrote down everything that they needed. If the items were in the store below, like diapers, wipes, food, cleaning supplies, or other items, Tina gave them to the Partners, at no cost. If H-E-B didn't sell the item, Tina was equipped with gift cards, hotel rooms, clothing, etc. Anything that the Partners needed, H-E-B took care of.

In Tina's words, "I never once asked anyone for proof of loss. They didn't need to show me a picture or proof. I thought this is how I want to live. We're not only helping, we were trusting. And the attitude was, don't worry about the one person who's going to take advantage of you, take care of 99 percent that are telling you the truth."

This experience was so impactful that Tina James decided she wanted to make her career at H-E-B. Her sense of purpose was aligned with the company and she knew she wouldn't experience that elsewhere. Tina stayed with the company for over 30 years.

Fast forward twenty years, and the United States was beginning to understand that COVID-19 was going to be a big deal, but H-E-B had already been preparing for months. Accustomed to being there for their communities and Partners during natural disasters, H-E-B crisis management had mobilized. But this was not a hurricane, flood, or tornado. This was a business-making or breaking event. When their leadership team understood this wasn't going to be the norm, the top five, including Tina, got together and hatched a plan to move forward with lighting speed. At the center of this plan was their Partners. H-E-B understood the assignment. To be a purpose driven organization, it must be purpose driven in bad times and in good.

During this same time, I was working in Central Market, a high end grocery store that is a part of the H-E-B family, and it was truly interesting to watch what was going on. Many customer-facing industries were understanding that long gone were the days where a company could stay neutral on political issues. 2020 demanded that companies take sides in areas like mask or no mask, doing temperature checks on employees, social justice, etc. Companies that had a strong purpose and understood their values were able to find their true north quickly. It was my honor to be a Partner with H-E-B and see this happen very quickly, and on a massive scale. On the other hand, companies that did not have a purpose were playing catch up. So we can see how important a purpose is, but what is it, truly? And how does it differ from mission and vision?

What is the difference between purpose, mission, and vision?

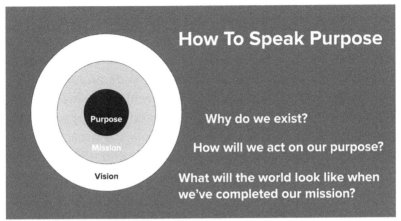

Image used with permission from https://davidburkus.com/2020/05/whats-the-difference-between-vision-mission-and-purpose/

Let's look at these concepts further.

Mission: Defining What the Organization Does

A mission statement serves several purposes for an organization.

It defines what an organization does, how it does this, and who it serves. It is a concise statement that focuses on the present and describes the organization's core purpose and goals. A mission statement should be clear, easy to understand, and reflect the organization's values and principles.

Declaring what the organization does, helps stakeholders understand the organization's purpose. It sets the tone for decision making and helps guide the organization's actions. A mission statement can help differentiate the organization from competitors and attract customers and employees who share the organization's values.

For example, the mission statement of the Walt Disney Company is "To entertain, inform and inspire people around the globe through the power of unparalleled storytelling, reflecting the iconic brands, creative minds and innovative technologies that make ours the world's premier entertainment company."[8] This mission statement captures the essence of what Disney does every day, in the present—provide entertainment through storytelling—and highlights the company's commitment to creativity and innovation.

Vision: Defining Where the Organization Wants to Go

While the mission statement defines what the organization currently does, the vision statement defines where the organization wants to go. It is a forward-looking statement that describes the ideal state the organization hopes to achieve. A vision statement should be inspiring, motivating, and reflect the organization's values and beliefs.

A vision statement serves several purposes for an organization. First, it provides a clear and inspiring picture of where the organization is headed, which helps stakeholders understand the organization's long-term goals. Second, it helps align stakeholders around a common goal and motivates them to work towards achieving that goal. Finally, a vision statement can help attract customers and employees who share the organization's values and beliefs.

For example, the vision statement of Microsoft is "Empower every person and every organization on the planet to achieve more." This vision statement reflects Microsoft's commitment to empowering people and organizations through technology, and sets a lofty but inspiring goal for the company to work towards.

Purpose: Defining Why the Organization Exists

While the mission and vision statements define what an organization does and where it wants to go, the purpose statement defines why the organization exists in the first place. It is a statement of the organization's fundamental reason for being, and that impact it has on the world. A purpose statement should be inspiring, motivating, and reflect the organization's values, beliefs, and principles.

A purpose statement does several things for an organization. First, it provides a clear and inspiring statement of the organization's reason for being, which helps stakeholders understand the organization's impact on the world. Second, it helps align stakeholders around a common purpose and motivates them to work towards achieving that purpose. Finally, a purpose statement can help attract customers and employees who share the organization's values and beliefs.

For example, the purpose statement of Patagonia is, "We're in business to save our home planet." This purpose statement reflects Patagonia's commitment to environmental sustainability, and sets a bold and inspiring goal for the company to work towards.

Key Differences Between Mission, Vision, and Purpose

While mission, vision, and purpose are all important concepts for leaders, they each serve a different purpose:

1. Mission statements focus on the present and define what the organization *does*, how it does this, and who it serves.
2. Vision statements focus on the future and define where the organization *wants to go* and what it hopes to achieve.
3. Purpose statements define *why* the organization exists and its impact on the world.

Another key difference between these concepts is the time frame they cover. A mission statement is focused on the *present* and is typically more concrete and specific than a vision or purpose statement. A vision statement, on the other hand, is focused on the *future* and is typically more aspirational and inspiring than a mission or purpose statement. A purpose statement is focused on the fundamental reason for the organization's existence and its impact on the world, and is typically more broad and abstract than a mission or vision statement.

It's also worth noting that these three concepts are interconnected and can influence each other. A clear mission statement can help inform the organization's vision and purpose, while a compelling vision and purpose can help motivate stakeholders to work towards achieving the organization's mission.

In addition, it's important to ensure that these statements are aligned with each other and with the organization's values and principles. When these statements are aligned, it can lead to clarity and direction within the organization.

While these three concepts may seem similar, they are distinct and serve different purposes. A clear and concise mission statement defines what the organization does, while an inspiring vision statement defines where the organization wants to go. A purpose statement defines why the organization exists and its impact on the world.

By understanding these concepts and ensuring that they are aligned with each other and with the organization's values and principles, leaders can provide a clear direction and sense of purpose for their organization. This can help motivate stakeholders to work towards achieving the organization's goals and create a strong and successful organization.

How do you make purpose personal?

We have been talking about a company's purpose in general, but not so much in relation to the individual. We know what it feels like to work at a company where our purpose aligns with the company's, but we don't spend a lot of time being intentional about making our purpose personal for us or our teams. We heard from Tina earlier about how purpose changed her entire family's trajectory. That is the power of making purpose personal. But how does a leader do it? It can feel overwhelming, but when it is broken down into parts, it is what good leaders are already doing.

The first step in connecting purpose to the personal is understanding that our brains are hardwired to give. The more we can identify with someone, like our customer, the more we feel like helping them. That was one of the lessons that we would see first hand working at Walt Disney World. When a Guest would come in and start throwing a fit, we would do the minimum of what was required to take care of the situation and move them along. When a Guest would come in and confide in us, sharing their challenges, disappointments, etc., but still treating us as human, we would move mountains for them. Humans are apt to give more and work harder when we can identify with the person we are tasked to help.

A few years into my career, we had a Cast Member who joined us, and had extensive retail experience with big box retailers. We felt like they *should* have been amazing. We quickly realized that the expectation wasn't lining up with reality. This is where purpose showed up. You see, this Cast Member had worked with budget big boxes before and was trained to save money at all costs. The purpose of the big box was to get a large assortment of items out at the lowest cost possible. This was a direct contradiction of what we learned at Disney. As much as that Cast Member wanted to succeed, they could not align their internal values with that of Disney's. Where we were creating magic by giving away a shirt or other item, they saw it as wasteful and harmful to the organization. That Cast Member didn't last long unfortunately. Purpose has nothing to do with skill set, and everything to do with how a person views what is important to them.

USAA, who is known for its amazing personalization and empathy, is another great example of this. This is because, in order to better understand the unique military background of their customers, thousands of USAA employees have gone through mock boot camps, complete with drill sergeants and physically demanding tasks. This unique training not only helps employees understand the culture of the military and the demands on customers, but introduces them to the mindset of a USAA member, making things more personal. A large number of USAA employees are also military veterans, which gives them an accurate perspective on what products and services military families need most.[9]

This is an example of a company that is connecting the dots for their employees. They are taking what already exists in their employees, and helping them to understand how to connect it to what the company does. This is how you personalize "purpose." But let's break it down into key steps.

Spend time with your employees.

The first thing that can help uncover your employees' purpose is to spend time with them. During one on one's, ask them what gets them excited outside of work. Pay attention to the stories they share with you. Are they about family, volunteer work, friends? All of these snapshots into their personal lives will help uncover their values and their purpose.

We had a Cast Member, we will call him Don. He worked in a stock inventory role while I was working in resorts. Every Monday, he would come in and have loads of stories to share about his grandkids who were all under the age of ten. He would have picture after picture of their soccer games, birthday parties, and outings. It was obvious that his world revolved around his grandkids. He was amazing at his job and a joy to be around... most of the time.

For some reason, Don had no patience when it came to the college kids that would join us on the Disney College Program. He would get frustrated and irritable, and many times would snap at them. The first couple of times, we talked about it, and he said he would get better. He didn't. Then one day I walked into work just in time to see him go off on one of our newer Cast Members. I was furious! When

I spoke to him, he was defensive and angry. He knew he was in trouble, and he wasn't going to go down without a fight. At that moment, I thought of his grandkids. I asked him what he would do if he walked in and saw someone talking to one of his grandkids the same way he had just spoken to that young man.

Almost immediately I could see his shoulders slump and he looked down. When he looked back up, the fight was gone and he said, "I get it, it won't happen again." He went back to work and I sat there thunderstruck. After all of the conversations, all of the heated discussions threatening to discipline, all it took was connecting to his purpose and values, for him to understand how he was showing up in a way that went against what he believed.

That is the power of purpose. Without spending time with him, looking at the pictures, and hearing about the soccer games, I wouldn't have been able to connect the dots. Too many times, leaders get caught up in the emergencies and we forget to lay the groundwork with our teams. The groundwork is what gives us the ability to personalize conversations, coaching sessions, and "purpose."

Use feedback to align to purpose.

Another way to personalize purpose is in the delivery of feedback. When is the last time you have given someone specific and positive feedback? Too often we save feedback for when someone is screwing up. If you see a behavior that you want repeated, highlight the behavior, say thank you to the person, and help them connect that behavior to their "purpose." It was not uncommon for a Disney leader to end a positive feedback conversation with, "Thank you for making magic." By using these words, Cast Members knew exactly what magic looked like and how to repeat it in the future.

Attracting, Hiring and Retaining Talent for Purpose

A prime example of when purpose comes into play is for the Southwest #KeepDean campaign that happened at the beginning of covid. In the words of Mike Kulkulski, former Southwest Captain, "Dean Jamous...is the most junior Pilot on the SWA seniority list today. The Save Dean campaign... means no one gets furloughed... [The] Pilots of Southwest will do everything in our power to prevent furlough in the true spirit of our predecessors. That is what it means to be a Southwest pilot."[10]

Dean would have been the first pilot to get furloughed had Southwest needed to begin furloughs. The pilot community worked together to protect all of the pilots. This is purpose in action. If Southwest's purpose is people, they damn well better show up when times get hard. And that is the thing about purpose. It is easy to say a company has a purpose when everything is going great. But when things get tough, when you have to choose what you want your team, your brand, your products, your company, to stand for. That is when you will identify your true purpose. For any organization, the employees are watching during moments of strife to see if the purpose that has been given to them is upheld or put to the wayside.

We have covered why purpose is so critical. According to Forbes, consumers are increasingly making purchase decisions based on what a brand stands for.[11] Nicholas Pearce, author and professor, sums it up: "Purpose is engaging in the radical act of connecting our souls with our roles." But how do we get our team involved? Slowly and intentionally, is the answer.

When considering purpose, many times, it is a fluffy or nebulous idea. Consider what I was taught at Disney- "We make magic." That is a great purpose, it gives you all the feels! But how do you actually make magic? That was the challenge that leaders had. We needed to be able to break down this big, fluffy concept into something concrete and actionable. There were a multitude of ways we could do this. The important thing for us to realize was that it didn't just start once we hired a new Cast Member. It started during the hiring process, and it never stopped.

Hiring for purpose:

When an organization is purpose driven, they need to start looking at purpose before a candidate is ever on the payroll. The organization needs to be clear what they are looking for regarding purpose driven behaviors. Technical skills can be taught, soft skills are a lot harder.

When I was working in healthcare, we had gone through a phase where we were desperate for certified nursing assistants. It is an extremely hard job with extremely low pay. Getting people in and keeping them had proven very difficult for a spell, so the company had been lax when hiring. They were essentially hiring anyone who was certified. This was causing some issues for the center because we were getting a lot of individuals who were not team oriented, and very focused on themselves. The CNA's needed to be able to work together for things like lifting patients, emergencies, or if they got behind.

We were talking about it during a leadership meeting and I suggested hiring for team work instead of the hard skills. We decided that during the interview process, a candidate would be given a tour of the facility by another CNA. While they were touring, an employee of the facility would "accidentally" spill something. Our theory was that team oriented individuals would stop to assist while those who were more task or self oriented would continue on with the tour. This theory turned out to be accurate. We were able to start bringing in CNA's that were focused on the team versus themselves. We wouldn't have been able to do this if we weren't first clear on what we are looking for.

To become clear on purpose, ask yourself what the organization's purpose is. Then think of the employees who live into the purpose. What behaviors are they doing that leans into the purpose? What behaviors exist that take away from the purpose? A purpose can be operationalized with a little thought and intentionality. That is why it was not uncommon to have Guests walking around Disney a little bit in awe. Because what they experienced, the small details of magic, were consistent.

A little girl walking around dressed up as princess would be greeted with, "Hi Princess" throughout the day.

A young boy walking around dressed up as a pirate would be greeted with, "Arrrgggghhh Matey."

Someone having a bad day? Have a free Mickey Bar.

A bird stole your Turkey Leg? Have another.

All of these are examples of a purpose that has been oper-ationalized. What do you have in your organization that is a physical example of living into your purpose? Now look for those traits in the interview process and ask questions that help you uncover them.

Once they have been hired:

Lee Cockerell, retired executive vice president of opera-tions for Walt Disney World says, "Starting their first day, and every day after, let them know you care. Connect with them, invest in them, and value them from the beginning. Make them part of the process and help them understand they matter. Create an environment that appreciates and equips people. Then be intentional about implementing it. Be purposeful about building trust. Hiring and retaining the right people is an area good leaders pay attention to."[12]

CHAPTER 5

HOW TO CREATE A PURPOSE WHEN YOUR ORGANIZATION DOESN'T HAVE ONE

Purpose is all well and good, you might be thinking. But what if your organization doesn't have a purpose? Or it has a purpose, but it is hard to translate to the front line? Then, as leaders, we have to get creative. While working at Central Market, we had another challenge. On day one of orientation, the new employees would show up entirely lacking excitement. They worked at a grocery store. What was sexy about that?

They had not been with us long enough to see how the bigger purpose related to them, so we had to break it down.

This was done through the power of storytelling.

Imagine you are a new employee. You would be introduced to an imaginary customer, let's say her name was Alice.

Alice was coming into the bakery in a panic because the birthday cake she had made for her four year old daughter had collapsed and she needed something in less than three hours. You, feeling empowered and fresh out of orientation, would help Alice figure out her options and have her walking away with a cake that will make her daughter proud, all in less than thirty minutes. Total mom win!

A few weeks would pass by and you are walking through the store on the way to the breakroom when you see Alice standing in the baking aisle, holding two bags of chocolate chips, with a far away look on her face. You stop to talk to Alice and see tears in her eyes. Alice shares that her mom has recently passed and she wanted to make the chocolate chip cookies her mom made when she was having a bad day, because she was having a really bad day. But she didn't know what brand of chocolate chips her mom used in the recipe.

What is the one common ingredient in human gatherings? Food.

As a grocery store employee, you experience the highest of highs and the lowest of lows with our customers including birthdays, weddings, anniversaries, deaths, divorces, or loss of a job. The full range of human emotions take place here and you have to navigate that with class and grace. That is your new purpose, not selling groceries, but helping the customers navigate their highs and lows.

You see, purpose should be tied to an emotion. If your company's purpose is to improve shares for shareholders, your employees' purpose is a paycheck. Nothing more, and nothing less. The ability to translate the purpose for your team is a leader's super power.

So let's dig into how we do it.

Uncover Your Team's Purpose

At first glance, trying to determine your team's purpose can be overwhelming. The purpose feels so big! But your team is probably already living into it, they just haven't put it into words.

What gets your employees excited?

What gets your customers excited?

If you receive surveys from your customers, read them and look for common threads. Think about what you do that helps to alleviate the pain of your customers. Remember, we identify customers as internal or external. A customer isn't just someone who spends money in your organization. If you are HR, your customers are the managers and teams you support. If you are marketing, your customer is the team you are creating for. So think about the customer you support and ask yourself, what is the pain that we can alleviate? Keep drilling in, keep asking why. One of my favorite tools for this is the "five whys". You start by asking a question and when you get an answer, you ask why. You do this up to five times. Generally, when you can't ask why anymore, you are pretty close to your answer, or in this case, your purpose.

I asked ChatGPT to help us out with an example. I will include the prompt in case you want it to help you out as well.

Prompt: Use the Five Whys methodology to uncover an internal HR team's purpose

1. Why does the HR team exist in our organization?
   - The HR team exists to manage the human resources and support the well-being and development of employees.
2. Why is it important to manage human resources and support employee well-being and development?
   - A well-managed workforce with satisfied and engaged employees leads to increased productivity, higher employee retention, and a positive work environment, ultimately contributing to the success of the organization.
3. Why is increased productivity, higher employee retention, and a positive work environment essential for the organization's success?
   - These factors directly impact the organization's ability to achieve its goals, maintain a competitive edge, and foster a strong company culture, which in turn attracts and retains top talent.
4. Why is having a competitive edge and strong company culture important?
   - A competitive edge and strong company culture enable the organization to innovate, adapt to market changes, and maintain long-term growth and profitability. They also contribute to the organization's reputation, which can affect its ability to secure clients, customers, and partnerships.
5. Why do we need to ensure long-term growth, profitability, and a good reputation?

- Ensuring long-term growth, profitability, and a good reputation is vital for the organization's sustainability, its ability to create value for stakeholders, and its capacity to make a positive impact on the communities it serves.

After asking the Five Whys, it becomes clear that the internal HR team's purpose is to manage and support employees to manage and support employees, by fostering a positive work environment that encourages productivity and retention. This, in turn, contributes to the organization's competitive edge, long-term growth, and reputation, ultimately enabling it to create value for its stakeholders and positively impact the communities it serves.

Another way to put this could be, "The purpose of the HR Team is to ensure sustainability for the organization, its stakeholders and the community we serve by supporting the employees and leaders to increase satisfaction, productivity, and engagement."

I asked ChatGPT to help us make the purpose a little more inspirational. It is a little long for my taste, but I wanted to share so you could see an alternative.

"The purpose of our HR Team transcends the usual. We are not merely a department; we are the stewards of the organization's soul, the guardians of its future. We exist to cultivate a flourishing landscape for the organization, its stakeholders, and the broader community we passionately serve. We stand as a nurturing beacon for our employees and leaders, fostering an environment where satisfaction and productivity bloom alongside commitment and engagement. We inspire the growth of individual potential, sparking the synergy that fuels our collective momentum towards sustainable excellence. We are the wind beneath the organization's wings, quietly strengthening its flight towards higher realms of success, and etching a positive mark in the communities we touch. Our purpose is to let each and every member of our organization know - we don't just work for today, we inspire and build for an extraordinary tomorrow."

It is definitely inspirational!

Once you get this far, it is time to personalize what your team does and what makes it unique. Uncovering your team's purpose isn't a quick exercise. And it isn't meant to be uncovered solo. It is helpful to get it started, then bring your team in. Let them take it to the final steps.

The purpose will most likely be a work in progress and continue to be refined until your team is able to articulate why they do what they do, and the difference that it makes. (If you want help uncovering your purpose, email me: summer@summerjelinek.com. I love this stuff!)

Start, Stop, Continue

Once you have gotten closer to identifying your team's purpose, let's look at how to operationalize it. A powerful and underutilized tool for helping to reinforce purpose is the, "start, stop, and continue" method. This exercise consists of three parts that you and your team can do together.

Start

When considering your purpose, identify new actions or behaviors that should be introduced. These could be new initiatives, processes, or practices that are believed to have a positive impact on the team's performance, employee satisfaction, or alignment with the organizational purpose. In other words, what does your team need to start doing to live into the purpose you all agreed upon?

Stop

When considering your purpose, assess existing actions, behaviors, or practices that are not adding value, or may be counterproductive. These could be outdated processes, ineffective communication channels, or any other practices that hinder the organization's progress or detract from its purpose. The goal of this step is to eliminate or modify these practices to improve overall performance.

Continue

When considering your purpose, identify actions, behaviors, or practices that are currently effective and should be maintained. These are aspects of the organization or team that contribute to its success and are aligned with its purpose. The goal is to reinforce and support these practices to ensure their continued success.

The purpose of the, "start, stop, and continue" method is to begin highlighting behaviors that reinforce or take away from the purpose. A purpose is only an idea until a person is able to understand what actions to take to bring that purpose to life. Think back to the Harry Potter example I shared earlier. My purpose was to *make magic, period.* But what does that actually look like?

In the case of that story, it meant partnering with a competitor when Disney couldn't create the magic that the family needed.

Once you have the behaviors that reinforce the purpose, then you begin crafting the culture.

Crafting a Purpose Driven Culture

Purpose is an organization's fundamental reason for existence, but the culture is the set of shared values, beliefs, norms, and behaviors that shape the way employees interact with one another and approach their work. The two, purpose and culture, should be working together hand in hand. Culture is what happens when the manager is not in the room. When you are building out behaviors that influence and reinforce the purpose, consider what already exists within the culture. Culture is one of the easiest things to let happen, but one of the hardest things to be intentional about. Why is it so hard though?

1. Embracing diversity: Our individual values, beliefs, and experiences are beautifully unique, but these differences can also make it challenging to build a culture that speaks to everyone's hearts. It's a complex journey to find common ground and cultivate a shared understanding.

2. The dance of time and change: Culture isn't born in a day. It's a slow, steady process where values, beliefs, and practices are shared, embraced, and passed down through generations. And as the world around us changes, so does culture—it's a living, breathing entity that grows and evolves with us.

3. The invisible threads: Culture is often woven from the intangible and unspoken, or the things we know but can't always put into words. This elusive nature makes it difficult to pinpoint and communicate the very elements that form the fabric of a new culture.

4. The courage to let go: Change can be scary, especially when it involves cultural norms and values that are etched into our identities. To create a new culture, we must be brave enough to step out of our comfort zones and release the familiar customs that no longer serve us.

5. Connection through communication: Building and nurturing a culture requires authentic communication. Yet, language barriers, cultural misunderstandings, and varied communication styles can create hurdles in conveying and maintaining the essence of our cultural vision.

6. The power of leadership: A thriving culture needs strong, committed leaders who can guide, inspire, and sustain its vision. Without such leadership, creating a cohesive and lasting culture becomes an uphill battle.

7. Navigating external forces: Cultures aren't immune to the world around them. Political, economic, technological, and social shifts can shape and influence a culture's development and sustainability, making it all the more challenging to create a stable and enduring cultural identity.

In short, when you are trying to influence a group of individuals to act together, you have to take into account all of the things influencing the individuals, and it is a lot.

But what happens when you get it right? We see it every day in organizations that have a strong culture. They are able to fall back on it to help guide them in moments of challenge. As discussed before, this is what H-E-B did when COVID hit in 2020. As a former employee of H-E-B, I speak from firsthand experience, they showed up for us when we were terrified. They ensured we had what we needed to be able to do our jobs to the best of our abilities. It wasn't always pretty, but we did it.

When the social unrest around the George Floyd murder occurred, they showed up again in a very decisive way. If the purpose of H-E-B was people, and the culture was people first, how could they not show up? At every turn, they were able to make the hard decisions because they knew what the culture demanded of them. I was, and still am, very proud to have been a Partner during these times, not only for how they took care of us, but also for how they showed up consistently, living into the purpose, mission, and vision, even when it was hard. *Especially* when it was hard.

This is the power of culture and purpose. Together, they are the torch and the compass during difficult times. Can you find your way with just one, the torch or the compass?

Yes, but it is so much easier with both.

CHAPTER 6

MAKING SURE TALENT AND PURPOSE ARE ON THE SAME TEAM

I n the realm of effective leadership, there exists a truth that should never be overlooked or underestimated: the importance of aligning talent to purpose. This notion, which resonates deeply with my research and beliefs, reveals a fundamental aspect of successful leadership. That is the ability to bring together the unique strengths and passions of individuals with a common vision, which ultimately leads to extraordinary achievements.

Aligning talent to purpose is not a mere act of matching job descriptions with skills or qualifications. It goes far beyond that surface-level approach. It requires leaders to understand the organization's purpose, their individual purpose, and the purpose of their team, to then delve into the essence of what drives individuals, their innate talents, and their aspirations. It calls for an understanding that people are not mere cogs in a machine, but rather, individuals with unique perspectives, experiences, and contributions to offer.

When you consider an industry like retail, the job is pretty consistent from store to store. Matching talent to purpose is where the brands really begin to differentiate themselves. This was extremely apparent when we were trying to hire people for Walt Disney World retail. You have heard all about our purpose–to make magic. Magic isn't cheap y'all. There has to be a willingness to create that magic. We struggled when individuals would be hired from low cost big boxes. The essence of the job was the same, but the purpose was very different. If a person found value and purpose in help-ing to keep costs down as much as possible at the low cost big boxes, they would struggle to give away a $90 dress at Disney. Neither of these, saving money or making magic, is necessarily wrong, but the two purposes would struggle inside of the same organization.

To align talent to purpose means to recognize and value the multifaceted qualities that each individual brings to the table. It requires leaders to go beyond the surface and engage in genuine conversations that unveil the passions, values, and dreams of their team members. It is through this understanding that leaders can cultivate an environ-ment where individuals feel seen, heard, and valued— a crucial component of effective leadership.

When talent aligns with purpose, magic happens. Individuals feel a deep sense of connection and commitment to their work, which transcends the realms of mere obligation. They become more than just employees; they become passionate advocates and stewards of the organizational vision. They bring their whole selves to their roles, infusing their work with creativity, enthusiasm, and a deep sense of meaning. This is why we are drawn to those employees who radiate their purpose. As customers, we can see it and feel it. We can also see and feel when it is lacking.

But how does one accomplish this formidable task of aligning talent to purpose?

It begins with intentional recruitment practices that look beyond skill sets and delve into the values, passions, and potential for growth. It involves creating an inclusive and psychologically safe environment that nurtures diversity and encourages individuals to bring their authentic selves to work. It necessitates leaders to engage in ongoing conversations with their team members, providing feedback, support, and opportunities for growth. And it requires investing in professional development, and recognizing that by fostering the growth and advancement of individuals, the organization as a whole flourishes.

Moreover, aligning talent to purpose demands that leaders embrace their own authenticity. Leaders must be willing to show up authentically, to share their own vulnerabilities and fears, and to create space for others to do the same. By doing so, leaders foster an environment where trust flourishes, enabling individuals to fully embrace their talents and contribute meaningfully to the collective purpose.

In essence, aligning talent to purpose is an ongoing journey, an ever-evolving process that requires continuous effort, self-reflection, and adaptation. It demands that leaders create a culture that values individual strengths, encourages collaboration, and celebrates diversity. It involves taking risks and embracing failures as learning opportunities. It requires leaders to step into their authentic selves, lean into vulnerability, and challenge the status quo.

When I was working at Disney's Caribbean Beach Resort, we had a Cast Member, David. David bled pixie dust. He was absolutely made to work at Disney. David could also be a lot for the other Cast Members at times. He was "on" all of the time. He was always playing with the toys, or "merchantain-ing" as we called it. It was starting to cause some friction between him and some of the more subdued Cast Members. As a leadership team, we decided to partner with another hotel that was looking for concierge Cast Members. These Cast Members were more individual contributors and their job was to handle difficult situations and make magic. David was a perfect fit. He thrived in his new environment and created hundreds of moments of magic for the Guests that he would have been unable to do at the previous location.

When leaders embrace the power of aligning talent to purpose, they unlock the extraordinary potential within their teams. They create environments where individuals thrive, ideas flourish, and remarkable achievements become the norm. They embody the essence of effective leadership, an approach that acknowledges the human element, cultivates genuine connections, and inspires greatness.

Always a Recruiter

One of the first lessons I learned as a leader is to always keep an eye out for great talent. Working at Walt Disney World was a challenging job and finding the right people was the responsibility of everyone. Anytime we would go on vacation, or even out on a date, Miles knew that we would be going in and out of every retail location and gift shop. This was not necessarily to buy anything, but instead to check out the talent. My business card was always in my pocket and if I came across amazing talent, they got a business card with a quick message on the back telling them to contact me if they were interested. I started this simply because I wanted to share the amazing experience of being a Cast Member with others, but it developed into a requirement as the benefit for myself and my team became apparent.

I have spoken with many leaders who feel like doing this is poaching or stealing other people's employees. This is a common discomfort that leaders feel. What I suggest to them, I suggest to you as well: if that employee is happy, it will be very difficult to get them to leave. I am not suggesting aggressive recruiting (unless you are a recruiter). Instead, you are offering people opportunities to shift into a new position, if and when, the time is right for them. When you work for a company that you love, doing things you love, it becomes a motivator to share that with others. You want to bring them the same joy and passion you have discovered. You are not poaching, you are educating others on opportunities available to them.

I am not a recruiter, how do I recruit?

This is another challenge I get regularly. We all have the ability to recruit. Think about it, how often have you spoken to a friend or family member who was complaining about their job, and you told them all of the amazing things that happen at yours, and why they should work there? We naturally recruit when we are comfortable in our environment. It is trying to recruit when you are at another workplace that makes it tricky. Recruiting for hospitality was always the hardest. The frontline employees rarely had LinkedIn and their leaders were normally on the floor with them. This required a little bit of creativity. I have wrapped my business card with a quick message in a dollar bill and passed it to them as a tip. I have left info on a napkin, on the receipt, and if the option is there, had a quick conversation.

In an office environment, it can be easier, but still not easy. Below are five tips to get you started. Each of these tips require consistent use to be effective. Don't try something one time and then decide it will never work. Whether you are a full time recruiter or a leader trying to fill spots on your team, recruiting is a numbers game.

1) Know Your Employer Brand: You may not work in the marketing department, but you know why you choose to work with your employer. Be able to share this with others. Look at what is being said about your employer on Glassdoor. Pay attention to recognition your employer receives that would be important to future employees. Be able to speak to this in a quick elevator pitch. It should be no more than a minute or two.

2) Ask Your Employees: Your employees will also know what is, and is not good about working for your organization. Ask them if they know anyone who would be a good fit. Reach out to their suggestions and begin building relationships.

3) Join an association: there are associations for everything. From pet obesity to therapeutic humor to renaissance martial arts, there is truly an association for everything. Find an association that makes sense for you professionally and join it. You will meet

individuals who share similar passions and skill sets and will widen your network. If and when the opportunity arises that you need to bring on a new individual to your team or organization, you may already have someone in mind.

4) Go to industry conferences: this one is similar to the association. When you go to industry conferences you have the opportunity to meet other professionals in your industry. You widen your network and you build relationships with individuals that may be an amazing fit for your team.

5) Utilize social media: social media can be an incredible platform when looking for talent. Don't just leave it to the recruiters, get involved. Build your brand on platforms such as LinkedIn. Connect with individuals and professionals in your line of work or that have appropriate skill sets. Get creative. Join discussion boards and chip in on the conversations. Be active on the platforms that make the most sense. Don't wait until you need someone to get involved and start posting. And don't assume that your posts aren't receiving attention just because they aren't getting likes or comments. I can't tell you how many times I have gone to speak at a conference and someone has approached me that has known me due to my social media presence. They have never interacted with what I have posted, but do when they see me in person. Then I got an amazing story about how one of my posts was exactly what they needed to hear and how it drove them to make a decision they had been avoiding. I love those interactions! And they rarely have anything to do with likes or comments.

What do I do about the people that already work on my team?

As we discussed earlier, when you are trying to align talent to purpose, it is important to have intentional conversations with those that report to you. The amount of people on your team will determine how often you can meet with them. If you have four people, meeting with them every two weeks for a half hour or so is a reasonable request. If you have a team of 100, that isn't quite so reasonable.

However many people you have, be intentional about scheduling time with them and then talk to them about their passions and what gets them excited. In the conversations about work and their personal worlds, help them connect the dots between what they do and the purpose of the team. The thing about purpose is it can many times be vague. For example, "We make magic." Okay, great. What does that mean? How do you *behavioralize,* "we make magic?" It wasn't until we tied specific behaviors to this idea, and connected how they supported our purpose, that the Cast Members were able to understand.

As a leader at Central Market, we would explain to new employees that if a customer asked them which was better, the cheddar popcorn or the butter popcorn, the employee should open both bags up and let the customer try it. Then, if the customer really liked one, they should give the customer an unopened bag. This sounds great, but it was obvious that they didn't trust us when we said they could do it. After all, this wasn't their first retail rodeo. They knew that stuff like that could get you fired at other companies. So during orientation we would bring new employees to the floor and have them open up some products to sample with customers. It began to show that we really did value the experience we were giving our customers. If our customers wanted a normal grocery experience, they went to Kroger. If they wanted something exceptional, they came to Central Market. To be exceptional means to do things differently.

Help your employees understand what makes your organization exceptional and then help them understand how they can take specific actions to strengthen this.

Professional Development

This has always been one of my favorite comics. It is such an accurate portrayal of the tension between professional development and the reasoning behind not giving professional development.

First and foremost, let's acknowledge a fundamental truth: humans are wired for growth, evolution, and adaptation. Professional development is not a luxury, but an essential part of this journey. It's not a destination but a continuous process that involves learning, unlearning, and relearning. This is why it's a crucial element in aligning talent with an organization's purpose.

Organizations aren't simply structures; they are dynamic living systems. And their lifeblood? The talent that is within them, driving every initiative, every strategy, every mission. If an organization's purpose is its guiding star, then talent is the steering wheel, navigating through the complexities of competition, uncertainty, and change. Without continuous professional development, your employees will struggle to stay ahead of all of these complexities. The world is moving faster and faster, especially in business, and we cannot afford to slow down our learning.

The power of professional development lies in its ability to enhance not just the technical competencies of the team, but also to nurture the 'soft skills' like courage, empathy, creativity, and resilience, that drive innovation and foster collaboration. As Brene' Brown states in her research, vulnerability is the birthplace of innovation, creativity, and change.[1] By continually developing, we encourage vulnerability and foster courage in our teams. We learn to adapt, innovate, and lead in the face of uncertainty.

Professional development ensures we are not stuck in yesterday's success stories, and are ready to write tomorrow's narratives. It propels the evolution of talent in sync with the organization's purpose and the world's changing dynamics. It doesn't merely answer the question, 'What can you do?' It helps us explore, 'Who can you become?' And that's the essence of what we are trying to create as leaders—a space where we and our employees are able to be imperfect, change and evolve.

When professional development aligns with an organization's purpose, it infuses interactions with authenticity and relevance. Every individual and every team learns to navigate not by what is 'profitable' or 'popular,' but what aligns with their shared sense of purpose. They become less like employees following a job description and more like passionate contributors to a shared vision.

Professional development also encourages a culture of learning, a culture that sees failures not as proof of unworthiness, but as vital stepping-stones in the path of growth. A learning organization nurtures empathy, fosters connection, and promotes psychological safety, all critical elements in unlocking the highest potential of its talent.

Professional development isn't a cost. It is an investment. It is an investment in nurturing a culture of growth, learning, and innovation. An investment in fostering alignment between talent and purpose. An investment in fueling the continuous growth and adaptation that is at the heart of success. Because, at the end of the day, we aren't just building companies or teams or careers. We are building lives. And for lives to truly thrive, they must learn, grow, and evolve. Professional development is critical to this journey.

As leaders, one of our most powerful tools is to invest in our employees. Think about the last time you were offered the opportunity to go to a training or take part in a conference. How did you feel? Valued, honored, *seen*? Professional development allows you to support your team while also pouring into them in a way that is unique to the workforce. Stalled career growth was one of the top reasons cited for the Great Resignation.[2] Professional development is no longer nice to have. It is a must have.

When I was first building the "Magic" model, I told a coach what each letter stood for. He responded with, "Galvanize huh? You must have really been stretching for that G." I was offended. You see, the G had been chosen very specifically. Galvanize has two definitions. The first is to excite or shock someone into taking action. Diane had done this by getting us aligned on our purpose of, 'we make magic, period.'

The second definition is to coat iron or steel with a protective layer of zinc. My suggestion is that as leaders, we are responsible for both of these things. We are responsible to excite our teams into taking action, but also responsible for being the protective layer for them as they figure out what it means to live into their purpose. Too often we move immediately to discipline, instead of trying to understand where and why it went wrong, and educate the employee on what to do in the future.

Was Diane going to be the protective layer once she found out that I had charged $113.82 to our largest competitor? Let's find out.

The day had come. The Harry Potter family had received their magic. It was finally time to tell Diane that I had charged $113.82 to the Walt Disney World corporate card at Universal Studios.

To say that I was a little nervous about the conversation is an understatement. You see, I loved my job, and I really didn't want to be fired for this. So now we were going to truly understand, do *we make magic, period*? Or was that just a saying?

When I finally built up the courage to go and talk to her, I sat on the edge of the seat, straight up, nervous as can be. I'm pretty sure when I started talking, it was at a normal pace. But I know that by the end of it, Diane had a deer in the headlights look, and I felt I had broken the Guinness World Book of Records for the fastest speaker in existence.

I gave Diane very high level bits of information, as my frazzled brain tried to tell her the story and show just how important it was to this family. By the end of it, she was confused and I was out of breath. She used six magical words, "I think I need more information," and then started asking questions. She didn't get mad, she didn't fly off the handle, she simply asked questions.

When she finally got the story she needed, she said, "I wasn't there, you were. Was it worth it?"

I could barely whisper because of the tears that were in my throat, "Yes, it was worth it." She said, "That's all that matters then. Don't do it again, but well done."

I knew at that moment that I would jump off of a cliff for Diane, because she would be at the bottom to catch me.

And that is what it means to galvanize an employee. You create a safe space for them to grow and stretch and try new things and fail. But you do it in a way that they are not scared at the end. I knew that Diane was going to have to talk to our executive. The day of her meeting, I went up to her when she got back and said, "Hey, how'd the meeting go?"

She gave me a little smile and said "It went well".

"So, did you tell her about the charge?"

She said, "Yes."

"Did you get in trouble?"

She looked at me and said, "Was it worth it?".

"Yes ma'am, it was absolutely worth it."

She said, "Then don't worry about anything else."

And to this day, even though Diane and I still stay in touch, and she is still somebody I admire and respect to my core, I have no idea what happened when she told her executive. And I've come to understand that it's none of my business.

As a leader, our responsibility is to create this space, and then be the padding for the employee when things maybe don't go as planned. That's what Diane was for me that day.

So let's start breaking this down, to see how we can galvanize our employees even further.

CHAPTER 7

PSYCHOLOGICAL SAFETY - THE NEW FRONTIER OF SAFETY

D iane did an amazing job creating psychological safety for the team I was on during that time. We all adored her, and also knew that she wouldn't let us get away with anything. We felt confident holding each other and ourselves accountable to the team. As it generally happens when a leader is doing a phenomenal job, Diane was promoted and we got a new leader. This leader quickly made some decisions that impacted the team, not in a negative or positive way, but in ways we certainly felt. One of these decisions was to get new furniture. She did it without asking us and in the process, got rid of my chair. It was an old, ratty chair, but it was so comfortable. The new chairs looked nice, but were really uncomfortable. I, trying to be cute, hijacked a trophy from her office and wrote a ransom note that the trophy would get returned when a specific chair was ordered. It was all in good fun, but if I am being honest, also a little bit of a test.

Now that I am older, and hopefully a little wiser, I see the error of my ways. I take full ownership that this probably wasn't the wisest course of action. In the beginning, she handled it well. But then I started hearing rumors from my peers that she was talking about me with them, and not in the most flattering of ways. This was creating an us versus them situation. There were some other instances that occurred that quickly began to diminish the psychological safety we had as a team. When this leader would come in to begin her shift, she would walk to the gift shop and start pointing out everything that was wrong. There were no questions as to why it was in the shape it was in, no concern about call ins or emergencies, just blame. Within a few weeks, the team that I had loved felt disconnected and out of sync. It took years for us to feel safe together, but it only took weeks for it to go away. That is the power of psychological safety and the importance of knowing how to build, and maintain it as a leader.

What is Psychological Safety?

Psychological safety is a term that has become very popular recently, but what is it? As leaders, are we really responsible for our team's mental health? Yes and no. The Harvard Business Review[1] defines it as, "... a shared belief held by members of a team that it's OK to take risks, to express their ideas and concerns, to speak up with questions, and to admit mistakes—all without fear of negative consequences."

This definition is accurate for individuals as well. Think of the last time you made a mistake or took a risk. Were you confident that you would be treated fairly and respectfully? Or were you worried about an unkind reaction from your leader? These questions help us to uncover what it feels like to have or not have, psychological safety.

Psychological safety is the invisible yet palpable lifeblood of any healthy and productive organization. This might sound like a bold claim, but let's explore what it really means to foster psychological safety in the workplace and why it is a pivotal element in leadership, will help us understand the truth in this claim.

Psychological safety is not merely the absence of conflict or the promise of a stress-free environment. It is a shared belief that an individual is safe for interpersonal risk-taking. It is the assurance that one can express thoughts, make mistakes, and voice ideas or concerns without the fear of punitive repercussions.

In the context of leadership, we often speak of authenticity and vulnerability. Yet, these elements can only truly exist in an environment where psychological safety is established. It acts as the soil from which the seeds of innovation, creativity, and productivity can sprout.

If employees do not feel psychologically safe, they retreat into themselves, restraining their thoughts, ideas, and concerns. They may hesitate to report issues, suggest improvements, or contribute fully to team discussions. The collective intelligence of the team becomes muted, and the organization loses valuable insights and opportunities for growth.

One area that leaders have continued to struggle with is understanding that grit cannot be demanded, it must be cultivated. When an employee doesn't fear retaliation, they are more likely to take risks, be it in the form of asking 'stupid' questions, challenging the status quo, or admitting errors. This grit, which is a byproduct of psychological safety, is a vital ingredient for innovation.

Similarly, vulnerability, the act of opening up and showing one's authentic self, requires a safe environment. In a psychologically unsafe workplace, vulnerability is suppressed, and with it, human connection. The leader who can create a safe space for vulnerability fosters stronger relationships and builds trust within the team.

Creating psychological safety is not a one-time task, but a continuous process of cultivating trust and respect. It involves leaders modeling the behaviors they want to see, encouraging open communication, and handling mistakes as learning opportunities, rather than occasions for punishment or embarrassment.

When leaders establish psychological safety, they create a culture where every voice matters. A culture where employees feel valued and empowered, where they know their thoughts and ideas can make a difference. This fosters a sense of ownership and engagement, which not only contributes to a more positive work environment, but also boosts performance and productivity.

But there's more to it. An environment marked by psychological safety is also a space that respects and nurtures the whole person, not just the 'worker'. It acknowledges that we bring our entire selves to work— our emotions, our personal experiences, our fears and hopes. In such an environment, employees feel seen and heard, leading to improved well-being and job satisfaction.

Psychological safety is an essential cornerstone for a thriving, innovative, and resilient organization. It is where grit, vulnerability, and creativity are brought to light. It allows people to fully show up, engage, and contribute.

Leadership is not about control or authority. It *is* about creating an environment where others can excel. Psychological safety is, therefore, not just another HR term or a 'nice-to-have' element. It is a *must-have* for any leader aiming to build an inclusive, engaged, and high-performing team.

It may seem overwhelming to create this type of space. First, be intentional about creating it. Make decisions that enhance psychological safety, have uncomfortable conversations, and hold people accountable to how their words and actions impact others. Second, give yourself grace as you are going on this journey. If creating these spaces was easy, we would have a lot more of them. And finally, give your employees grace as you are creating these spaces. It will take time to build trust with them. Psychological safety is uncomfortable and people will come at their own pace. But it is worth it.

Let's build workspaces marked by psychological safety, where every individual can rise to their potential and where organizations can flourish. After all, the magic happens when we feel safe enough to step out of our comfort zones and stretch our horizons. Is safety and psychological safety the same thing?

When we think about safety in the workplace, our minds often go straight to physical safety. We visualize caution signs, ergonomic desks, and emergency drills. While physical safety is undoubtedly crucial, psychological safety is equally essential, but less visible.

In the past, physical safety was all that was meant when we talked about safety in the workplace. The concepts of psychological safety were foreign and "fluffy". Strong employees didn't need it, only the weak ones did. This created an environment where we have avoided saying when we need help, when we mess up, or when we are burnt out. There is a fear of being seen as weak. Current research shows that creating an environment of psychological safety is a game changer for teams.[2] It isn't a kryptonite, it is a super power.

Physical safety is about creating an environment free from physical harm or danger, a place where employees are not at risk of injury or health issues related to the work they do. It's about adhering to health and safety regulations, providing appropriate protective equipment, and maintaining a safe and healthy workspace.

Psychological safety, on the other hand, is about fostering a culture where employees feel secure and comfortable expressing their thoughts, ideas, and concerns without fear of humiliation, rejection, or retaliation. It is the bedrock upon which trust, open communication, and mutual respect are built.

These two aspects of safety are not mutually exclusive, but rather, complementary. Both are about respect for the individual and are necessary for a healthy, productive work environment.

Why, though, is psychological safety so essential in the workplace? Let's delve deeper.

Innovation, creativity, and problem-solving require us to move into uncertainty and risk. Courage, which is necessary for these actions, is not about the absence of fear but about choosing to act in the face of fear. Psychological safety allows for this action by creating an environment where employees feel safe to take risks, and where failure is seen as a stepping stone to learning and growth, not as a pitfall to punish or shame.

Without psychological safety, employees may hesitate to speak up, share ideas, or ask questions, especially when they perceive these actions to be potentially threatening to their image, status, or career. The result is a stifling of creativity and a brake on potential innovation.

Furthermore, psychological safety is intrinsically linked to authenticity and vulnerability. In a psychologically safe environment, employees feel comfortable showing up as their true selves, rather than wearing a 'professional mask'. They are more likely to engage in candid conversations, give and receive feedback constructively, and build stronger, more authentic relationships.

In contrast, a lack of psychological safety can lead to disengagement, decreased job satisfaction, and increased stress. It can fuel toxic behaviors like bullying or harassment, and even impact physical health. In other words, the effects of psychological safety, or the lack thereof, ripple out, and affect individuals, teams, and the organization as a whole.

Now, let's consider the role of leadership in this context. Leaders, through their behaviors and actions, have a profound impact on the psychological safety within their teams. When leaders model openness, admit their own mistakes, listen attentively, and treat failure as a learning opportunity, they contribute to a culture of psychological safety.

In essence, physical safety ensures that we don't get hurt on the job, while psychological safety ensures we feel safe to be our authentic selves, to learn, grow, innovate and contribute fully to our work. In a world that's increasingly complex and fast-paced, psychological safety is a necessity for thriving in the face of challenges and change.

Leadership, then, is not just about strategic plans and performance metrics. It's about shaping the culture, or the very atmosphere in which work is done. A culture of safety, both physical and psychological, is a catalyst for engagement, productivity, and innovation.

So, let's create workplaces that are safe in every sense of the word, where people feel seen, heard, respected, and valued. Let's create environments where vulnerability is honored, and every individual is empowered to bring their whole, authentic selves to work. Because that's where the magic happens. That's where we find the capacity to innovate, to solve complex problems, and to build robust relationships. That's where we unlock the true potential of our teams and our organizations.

Think of psychological safety as the foundation upon which a strong and resilient organization is built. In a psychologically safe environment, trust becomes the norm, and with trust, collaboration soars. Teams are more cohesive, more willing to share and pool their knowledge, and better equipped to navigate the complexities of modern work.

Remember, psychological safety doesn't mean avoiding tough conversations or difficult decisions. It is quite the opposite. It means creating an environment where these difficult conversations can happen in a respectful and productive manner. It's about holding each other accountable in a way that fosters learning and growth, not fear or resentment.

Here's the powerful truth: When people feel safe, they're more likely to step out of their comfort zones. They're more likely to take on challenging tasks, to learn new skills, or to offer innovative ideas. They're more likely to invest in their work and feel a sense of belonging and commitment to their team and organization.

In the end, both physical and psychological safety are about respect and care for the people who make up our organizations. It's about recognizing and honoring their humanity, their potential, and their worth.

Leading with a focus on safety, in all its forms, is a journey. It's a commitment to continuous learning, growth, and improvement. It's a commitment to creating an environment where each individual can thrive and contribute to their fullest potential.

Let's strive for workplaces that are not just physically safe, but psychologically safe too. Because when we do, we're not just building better workplaces, we're building a better world, where respect, authenticity, grit, and vulnerability are celebrated, and where everyone has the opportunity to be, and to become their best selves.

Remember, it's in our moments of vulnerability that we find our greatest strength. So let's step into those moments together, and create workplaces where everyone feels safe to do the same.

Psychological Safety and Innovation

Now, let's turn to innovation. Innovation is not born out of comfort and complacency but out of questioning, challenging, and experimenting. It's about venturing into the unknown, making mistakes, and learning from them. Psychological safety is the ground in which appropriate risk taking can grow.

When people feel psychologically safe, they are more likely to propose novel ideas, experiment with different approaches, and learn from failures. They are more likely to take the necessary risks that drive innovation. Without psychological safety, fear of criticism or punishment stifles this creative grit, putting a brake on innovation.

Let's consider the overall success of the organization. An organization is not just a machine made up of parts; it's a living, breathing organism made up of people, people with talents, ideas, emotions, and aspirations.

When these people feel psychologically safe, they are more likely to be engaged in their work, and more likely to stay with, and advocate for the organization. They are more likely to go the extra mile, contributing not just their skills and time, but also their enthusiasm, creativity, and commitment.

This, in turn, drives productivity, customer satisfaction, and ultimately, boosts the bottom line.

Moreover, psychological safety contributes to a positive organizational culture, one that attracts and retains top talent. In a world where talented individuals have many choices, culture is a key differentiator. A culture of psychological safety is a powerful competitive advantage.

Psychological safety is not an optional extra or a luxury. It's a key driver of team performance, innovation, and overall organizational success. It's a cornerstone of a healthy, vibrant, and resilient organization.

Leadership, therefore, is not just about setting goals and driving results. It's about creating an environment where people feel safe to be themselves, to express their thoughts, and to take risks. It's about nurturing a culture of trust, respect, and openness.

And when that happens, we're not just building better teams or better organizations. We're building a better world. A world where people feel seen, heard, and valued. A world where people are invited to dream, to innovate, and to be themselves.

Everything is moving so fast...

In Ed Catmull's book, *Creativity Inc.*, he shared a story of when Pixar animators were under extreme stress. It was after the release of the first *Toy Story*, and the studio was experiencing intense pressure to create a sequel that lived up to the success of the original. They had tight deadlines, and the attitude of the studio was "all in." They were working long hours, weekends, and pushing beyond normal boundaries. One morning, a husband and wife team came in after pulling an all-nighter. They were in a meeting a few hours later when they realized that their infant had not been dropped off at daycare. To their horror, they discovered that their baby had been left in the car. Thankfully, rescue workers were able to revive the baby, but that began a very intentional shift at Pixar. The parents and their teams, as well as Pixar leadership, understood that they couldn't keep pushing the way they had been. That level of burnout was toxic, and as the previous story showcased, dangerous.

It is hard for a company to take a look at the processes, both written and spoken, that could be causing harm, but Pixar did this with eyes wide open. Many times, especially in today's environment, being able to look at what you have always done as a leader, as a team, or as an organization, is critical to being able to uncover what is no longer working.

This is one of the scary parts of psychological safety. Everything is changing so quickly. As leaders in a society where it is just now becoming somewhat common to discuss feelings without being ostracized, we are expected to create entirely new cultures with individuals opening up more than ever before. We are walking a tightrope between creating a safe environment where everyone is free to be themselves, while also having an environment of accountability. It isn't easy, but the more you learn and the more you practice it, the easier it gets.

Aristotle, a famous Greek philosopher, says, "the whole is greater than the sum of its parts." This is why Google named their team project after him. The Aristotle project was Google's attempt to answer the question, "What makes teams work?" I am sure you can guess what their research found. The number one quality for effective teams was psychological safety.[3]

The ability to be vulnerable with a team, to share an idea without fear of ridicule or chastisement, is what is meant to be in a psychologically safe environment.

I want to be very clear about something. Psychological safety is not an absence of accountability. Accountability will be discussed further in the book, but being nice and polite is not psychological safety. Think of the best leader you have ever had, it could have been a coach, a teacher, a mentor, or a manager. If you think about this individual and think about whether or not they let you get away with things, you will see that they held you to a higher standard than you were accustomed to. But they also had the tools and resources to help you obtain the standards without making you feel like you were *lesser*. Individuals and teams strive in environments that have effective, respectful accountability, both for the teams and with the leadership.

How to Speak Up Without Getting Canceled

In my many conversations with other leaders, during training or after coaching sessions, I've encountered a pervasive fear of "getting canceled." It might be called something different, perhaps getting in trouble for saying the wrong thing, or not being politically correct, but it all comes down to the same thing. Leaders are scared to have difficult conversations because they don't want to say or do the wrong thing. While the accountability for those in power is much more public than it has ever been thanks to social media, the idea of getting canceled isn't something that is new. There are certain ways to approach difficult conversations and certain ways not to. Let's talk about the ways *to* approach the conversation first.

Approach the conversation before it becomes emotional.

One of the most common ways that leaders find themselves saying or doing the wrong thing is when they wait too long to have the conversation and find themselves angry or resentful of the employee. Say you have an employee who is fifteen minutes late every day. Each day you think to yourself that you need to say something, but something always comes up, or you don't feel like it. One day, you are relying on that employee to be on time for a big event. Every minute that ticks by you feel your blood pressure going up, your face getting red, the anger building. By the time the employee walks in, you are ready to explode. In this anger, you say something that can be taken personally. We have all been in this moment, where as soon as the words leave our mouth we know we made a mistake. Whether with an employee or a loved one, the words have weight, and can hurt the person that we threw them at. This is why it is so critical to have these conversations with as clear of a head as possible. When we get in front of the problem early, we are addressing a problem itself, rather than seeing the employee as a problem.

Prepare for the conversation

We would never go into a major presentation without practicing. Heck, most of us have to practice asking someone out on a date or saying "I love you" for the first time. We feel the pressure to get it right. When we are having difficult conversations, we should give it the same consideration. When you are having a conversation with someone that is a constructive or negative conversation, practice it beforehand. Spend some time talking it through with someone, write it down, or think through how the conversation is going to go. Be as in-depth as possible. Think of all of the ways the conversation could go sideways and prepare for those.

Your employee is not broken, so don't try and fix them

When you approach the conversation, do it with empathy and understanding. Keep your mind open to truly hear what the other person is saying. Don't go into the conversation thinking you *know* what happened. Your employee probably feels like they have a legitimate reason to do whatever they did. Your job is to try to understand the thought process behind it. You can only do this with an open mind, and by asking questions. You don't have to agree with them, but attempting to understand where they came from will make a huge difference in your employee feeling heard versus blamed.

Check your biases

We all have biases. This is a side effect of being human. Our brains are wired to make complex decisions rapidly. Unfortunately this can sometimes cause us to make wrong assumptions about people without even realizing it. I was training a new manager a few years back, and I immediately disliked them with an intensity that was surprising. I knew this wasn't normal for me, and kept checking in with myself to figure out what it was. I tried to keep it from impacting the new manager's first day, but it was hard. Part of me wanted to just trust my gut and not like him. The other part of me realized something was off about this and kept digging to try and understand what was causing such a strong reaction. At the end of the day, when he leaned in to shake my hand, I realized where the intense dislike was coming from. He wore the same cologne as an ex boyfriend from a really bad relationship. I hadn't thought about this ex boyfriend in decades. I had dated him in my late teens, and my brain had filed away everything about him as dangerous, including how he smelled. When this new manager walked in smelling like my previous boyfriend, my brain immediately screamed danger and it showed up as an intense feeling of dislike for him.

This is how tricky our biases can be. We form biases around previous relationships, things we have been taught by our families and loved ones, by society, by movies, and so much more. We can be biased based on things like race, sexuality, gender, and more. Are you in a position of recruiting? Do you have a bias around ethnic names vs. European names? If you see an applicant with the name Shanequa, are you more likely to pass it over for Shannon?[4] What about a physically demanding job? Do you immediately look for a Brandon instead of a Brandy?[5] How about a candidate that walks in with a notebook that is your favorite sports team, have they just moved up to the front of the line?[6]

Until we check in with our bias and understand where we are more likely to have an unconscious bias we can show up in unintended ways that lead to detrimental outcomes.

Talk to the behavior, not your interpretation

When we give feedback, many times we start with our *interpretation* of what we saw, not what we *actually* saw. For example, say you have an employee who is interacting with a customer and keeps speaking over the customer. When you approach the employee to give them feedback, you tell the employee that they were being rude. Rude is an interpretation of the behavior you saw. The behavior itself was speaking over the customer, and not letting them finish their sentences.

We interpret behaviors based on the lenses we see the world through, and many times those lenses are inaccurate. Criticism based on your interpretation of a behavior can feel like a personal attack. Calling out the actual behavior is less personal. It also leaves the person you are giving feedback to with very little direction as to what you want them to do instead. If you are given the feedback of rudeness, the first question you have is "How was I rude?" That is because an interpretation of a behavior doesn't let us know what we did right or wrong, it just lets us know how the other person feels about it.

The role of a leader is to facilitate psychologically safe spaces and create room for difficult conversations. This can be scary and feel like we are walking on a tightrope, but it is a critical and necessary job of leaders. We can't avoid it simply because we want to. Leaders need to spend time with not only their employees, but getting out of their comfort zone. The way to minimize the chances of getting canceled is to educate yourself about people and cultures different from yours. Go to the employee resource group. If you are not a part of that group, go as an ally, to learn and listen. Employee Resource Groups have so much potential for growth for those that take advantage of them. If you are going as an ally, realize you are a guest. Go in and listen. It isn't your place to argue or debate someone else's experience. It is your place to go, be quiet, observe, and learn, so you can be a better ally outside of that environment.

CHAPTER 8

MYTHS OF ACCOUNTABILITY

Accountability tends to conjure up a lot of preconceived notions or myths. This chapter is about shining a light on those myths and uncovering the truth of accountability, and why it is a critical component of leadership.

After I had been with Walt Disney World for about six years, I was getting a little bored of retail. An opportunity to move back into restaurant work (my home and professional starting place) came up, and I jumped at it. Before Disney, I had worked my way up from a pizza delivery driver to a sous chef in various restaurants, but I had not worked in a front of house position. In this position at Disney, I was a front of house leader for a quick service restaurant. Think Panera Bread, Chipotle, or Starbucks. It had that kind of feel. A unique aspect of this restaurant was that we were not overseen by a chef team, so I got to put some of my back-of-house skills into place.

We had a Cast Member, Mary, who started before I came on board. Mary was an individual contributor and an extremely hard worker. She was quiet and focused and didn't have to be heavily managed. She did a great job the first time, every time. Because of this, the leadership team asked if she wanted to be promoted to a cook. She accepted, and as happens in most circumstances, she got the basic training of the job, but none of the nuances. She could make the food, but anyone who has worked in a kitchen understands that it is so much more than just that. When I arrived, the restaurant was struggling with things like timing, freshness of product, etc. After observing for a few weeks, one of the problems became clear. Mary was quiet. Not just a little quiet, like she didn't speak more than one or two sentences for an entire eight-hour shift. When a kitchen only has one cook, that cook is the heart of the kitchen. They control the flow, set the pace, and ensure everyone has what is needed to get the Guests their food. It was not uncommon to have multiple Cast Members calling out their needs to Mary at the same time. In a normal kitchen, the cook would call back what they heard to ensure it was accurate. In this kitchen, there was none of that. Orders were being missed, or coming out wrong, which would cause remakes and would extend wait times. The first time I brought Mary into the office to talk about this, we went through expectations and the need to do callbacks and keep communication flowing. And by we, I mean I. I talked, Mary listened.

We went back into the kitchen and what do you think happened? Nothing. Nothing happened. No communication, food still got messed up or missed, and Guests still got angry.

Round 2. I brought Mary back into the office, gave her feedback, asked what I could do to help, and got a sullen look back. She went back to the kitchen, but no change.

Round 3. I brought Mary back, gave her feedback and she got mad. Not slightly mad, like *I didn't know she could talk that loud,* mad. And one question she asked stopped me in my tracks. She asked why I was the only leader giving her that feedback. Why had no other leader given her that feedback? It was a valid question and one that she shouldn't have had to ask. I wasn't prepared for it and didn't want to throw my peers under the bus, so answered it the best I could. We finished the conversation with me apologizing while also letting her know that this was a non-negotiable. The communication had to pick up.

I worked with her a lot over the next few days, jumping in to assist and modeling how call backs would work. After a few days, I saw her shoulders go down, her frown start to diminish, and she would attempt a call back every once in a while. Every time she did, I would give her a wink and a smile. By the end of the week, she was tentative, but she was talking. A few weeks in, Mary was running that kitchen like a pro. It was *her* kitchen, and there was no doubt in anyone's mind about that. She quickly became one of the rising stars in the back-of-house. But I never forgot her question. Why had no other leader given her that feedback? I couldn't go back and fix that experience, but I could ensure it didn't happen again.

That was the first step to understanding that we all have ideas about accountability, what it looks like, when and how to do it, and those ideas are very different from person to person. Let's look at the top myths of accountability.

Myth 1 - Accountability is a synonym for punishment.

The most prevalent myth is the misconception that account-ability is synonymous with punishment, that it is the pro-verbial stick used to punish those who fail to toe the line. This conception is not just wrong; it's counterproductive and damaging.

At its heart, accountability is not about punishment, it's about empowerment. It's not about establishing a culture of fear, but rather, a culture of grit, authenticity, and trans-parency. As leaders, it's our job to communicate effectively, establish clear expectations, and to create a robust frame-work that enables individuals to understand and take own-ership of their roles.

One might wonder, if accountability is not punishment, then what does it look like in practice? Well, in the simplest terms, accountability is about leaning into tough conver-sations. It's about saying, "I see you. I hear you. I believe in your abilities, and I'm here to support you in your journey to meet the expectations we've agreed upon." It's about cre-ating an environment where mistakes are not punished, but learned from, and where individuals can grow, both person-ally and professionally.

We should always remember that people can't be held accountable in a vacuum. They need a clear understand-ing of their roles, responsibilities, and the specific expecta-tions attached to their work. This clarity is not merely about listing tasks in a job description, but also explaining the 'why' behind the expectations. This understanding provides a sense of purpose and fuels motivation.

A critical element in fostering this environment is open communication. This means having frequent, honest, and constructive conversations about how things are going, where they can improve, and how the team or individual can grow. It involves acknowledging and addressing issues as they arise, not waiting until they have spiraled out of control. Many times, leaders will not say anything because they don't have time, or it is something small, but the same issue happening again and again causes frustration and resentment on the leader's part. Until eventually, one day, the leader explodes and the employee is left wondering what the heck just happened. Keeping the lines of communication open, having timely conversations, and not shying away from difficult topics helps to minimize the chance of these outbursts happening. Open communication also means asking for, and being open to receiving feedback with grace, and then trying to learn from it.

It is crucial to note that accountability is not a one-size-fits-all formula. Every individual, every team, and every organization is unique. We need to be flexible and adjust our strategies based on the people involved, the tasks at hand, and the broader organizational culture.

Building a culture of accountability is not about exerting control, it's about fostering independence. It's about letting your team know that you trust them enough to take ownership of their work, to make mistakes, and to learn from those mistakes. This process is what transforms a group of individuals into a cohesive, dynamic, and productive team.

Myth 2 -
Accountability only matters when something goes wrong.

Accountability, when misconstrued, can often morph into something it was never intended to be—a punitive tool wielded only when things go wrong. This interpretation distorts the true meaning of accountability, leading to a culture where blame is the rule, not the exception. This is a culture where the fear of retribution overrides the grit to innovate, explore, and grow. This myth, this misconception, is a barrier to creating an environment of trust, learning, and shared success.

True accountability is not a reactive measure deployed only in times of trouble. It's a proactive and continuous process, an integral part of everyday operations, where expectations are communicated, performance is discussed, and feedback is exchanged regularly, and not just when performance falls short. This understanding of accountability shifts the focus from blame to learning, from punishment to development.

Picture a culture where, instead of the fear of accountability, there is a respect and appreciation for it. This is a culture where individuals lean into their responsibilities not out of fear, but out of a sense of ownership and commitment. Imagine a space where failure is not a cause for blame, but an opportunity for learning and growth. This is the culture we aspire to when we embrace true accountability.

To manifest this environment, we need to foster open, transparent, and ongoing communication within our teams. This includes discussing expectations openly, sharing constructive feedback routinely, and treating mistakes as learning opportunities. Instead of waiting for an annual review to discuss performance or letting problems fester, leaders need to provide real-time feedback and guidance. It's about creating a dialogue, not a monologue, and it's about making these conversations a normal, non-threatening part of our teams' routine.

But fostering this open communication is not enough. Leaders must lead by example, and demonstrate accountability in their own actions. When leaders admit their mistakes, ask for feedback, and show that they too are fallible, it helps to normalize this behavior within the team. It sends a clear message that we are all in this together, we all have room to grow, and we are all accountable.

One of the hardest times I had to put this into practice was when I chose a Cast Member, Ashley, to help rebuild the stock room for a new inventory management software Disney was implementing. This was a huge project with a lot of eyes on it. I knew we had the team to pull it off and was ecstatic when we were chosen to beta test the program. It was a lot of work, but we were up for it. I asked Ashley to do the rebuild. She was one of our top Cast Members, very detail oriented, efficient and just an all around badass. One day, I was reading through the parameters of the new processes and realized I had given Ashley the wrong directions. She was rebuilding the stockroom, with well over 30,000 pieces of product in it, based on very specific, and very wrong instructions that I had given her. She was over half way done. She had been working on it for almost a week.

Sweating, I walked into the stockroom, where she was sitting on the floor working on the lower shelves. I sat down on the floor next to her and gave her a weak smile. I then confessed everything. I explained that I had given her the wrong instructions and we would essentially need to start over. I apologized profusely and let her know if she wanted me to choose someone else, I would. If she wanted to stay, she could choose the resources she needed so we could still hit the timeline targets. She looked down at her hands, and my mind exploded with unhelpful thoughts like, "I am the worst leader ever", "she must hate me", "what did I do", "I shouldn't be a leader."

All of these thoughts happened in a split second and I could feel myself shrinking. Then Ashely looked up, smiled, and told me what she needed to be able to finish the project on time. She wasn't thinking how much she hated me, she was just thinking through the new information. Was she frustrated? Yes, we both were, but we had a job to do and it was time to get it done.

Admitting that I made a mistake, a huge mistake, was very uncomfortable. I felt so vulnerable in that moment. Even now, a decade later, thinking about it makes me cringe. But if we as leaders are not going to admit when we are wrong, how can we create the space that shows our employees that they can admit when *they* are wrong?

Creating a culture of accountability also involves building psychological safety within the team. This means creating an environment where team members feel safe to take risks, voice their opinions, admit mistakes, and ask for help without fear of retribution. It's about valuing grit over comfort and fostering an environment where vulnerability is seen as a strength, not a weakness.

In this kind of culture, accountability doesn't equate to blame, it equates to learning, growth, and shared success.

It's not a tool to instill fear, but a means to inspire, motivate, and empower.

Accountability is not a switch to be flipped on when things go wrong. It's a continuous journey towards individual and team growth. When we understand and embrace this, we move away from a culture of blame and towards a culture of shared success. This journey requires grit, vulnerability, and commitment from everyone involved. But it will start with first steps from the leader, from you, role modeling and showing what these ideas look like. When it is embraced, it becomes a driving force for individual growth, team cohesion, and organizational success. As leaders, we are the catalysts for this shift. We are the role models for accountability. And it's up to us to lead the way.

Myth 3 -
Holding Someone Accountable means Micromanaging

When discussing accountability, a common misconception surfaces. Oftentimes, we confuse it for micromanagement. Leaders, under the guise of keeping employees accountable, might find themselves spiraling into a cycle of controlling every minute detail of their team's work. The myth that accountability equates to micromanagement obscures the fact that genuine accountability is about empowering individuals and teams to take ownership of their tasks, not controlling their every move.

At its essence, micromanagement is fear-driven. It is rooted in a lack of trust in the team's abilities to accomplish tasks without constant supervision. Leaders were forced to confront this when work from home versus in the office became a hot topic. Organizations had been fighting against work from home for years, telling their employees that it couldn't be done. Now, when it was either work from home or go out of business, organizations were figuring out how to make it happen. But the leaders couldn't see what the employees were doing. They were insecure about this new working dynamic and wanted to make sure their team was doing "what they were supposed to." All of a sudden we see a boom in software that "monitors" the employees. I call this software, "gotcha software." Its purpose is to catch the employees doing something wrong. The software would count keystrokes, how long the employee was away from their desk, video surveillance, GPS tracking, and more. This is a prime example of micromanaging. Because the organizations were convinced that the employees were going to do something wrong, they built or brought in the "gotcha software" to catch them when the employee did something wrong.

Think back to what we learned about Emotional Intelligence. What does our brain do when we tell it that we think our employees are going to do something wrong? It finds them doing the "wrong things." Many times, the wrong things weren't wrong, they just didn't look the way we expected them to. The problem is that working from home completely rethinks the way work is done. Boundaries become fuzzy, and it doesn't look the same as it did in office. An employee may actually be working more hours at home, but the hours are split up, so there is a giant chunk of time in the afternoon that there is no work being done. The leader sees this via the, "gotcha software," and assumes the employee isn't working their full shift. The leader never thinks to look at other time slots such as, after the employee has put their kids to bed, to see the hours worked then. A 2022 study by the Harvard Business Review showed that monitoring employees actually made them *more* likely to break the rules, not less.[1]

Micromanagement, such as, "gotcha software," stifles creativity, reduces morale, and undercuts a sense of personal agency. On the contrary, authentic accountability springs from trust and respect. It's about setting *clear expectations* and equipping the team with necessary resources, then stepping back to let them navigate their work.

Leaders embracing true accountability cultivate an environment where employees feel empowered to take risks, make decisions, and exhibit their full creative potential. This doesn't mean there's no direction or guidance. Instead, leaders serve more as mentors, providing their team with the necessary resources, and offering support when needed.

This starts by setting clear expectations. It involves defining what success looks like and how it will be measured, providing a framework which the team can operate within autonomously. It means detailing the desired outcome, but allowing the team to chart their course towards it. This gives them the freedom to innovate, solve problems, and learn, promoting not only a sense of ownership but also a culture of continuous improvement.

Providing necessary resources is also a crucial part of this equation. Leaders must ensure their team has the tools, information, and support required to succeed. This includes creating an environment where asking for help is seen as a sign of strength, not weakness.

Then, leaders must step back, let go of the reins and trust their team to deliver. This doesn't mean they are uninvolved or distant. They should remain accessible and open, ready to offer guidance or help troubleshoot issues. But it's crucial to resist the urge to jump in and take over at the first sign of trouble. Leaders must give their team the space to stumble, so that they can learn and grow.

Empowering individuals and teams in this way demands vulnerability and grit. Leaders must be brave enough to let go of control and trust their team. They must be vulnerable enough to allow mistakes to happen and treat them as opportunities for learning, not as failures.

In a nutshell, true accountability is not about micromanaging every task. Instead, it's about nurturing a culture where individuals are trusted to take ownership of their work and are provided with the resources and support to excel. It's about striking a balance between providing direction and allowing autonomy. When leaders let go of control and lean into trust, they unlock a level of creativity, resilience, and performance that micromanagement could never achieve. This shift requires grit, trust, and vulnerability, but the rewards are worth it.

Myth 4 -
High Accountability Equals a Stressful Environment

A prevailing myth in many organizations is that high levels of accountability create a stressful work environment. It's the image of employees walking on eggshells, always anxious and worried about meeting expectations. This view reflects a fundamental misunderstanding of what accountability truly means, and it can lead to detrimental effects on team dynamics, morale, and productivity.

In reality, high accountability, when properly understood and implemented, is not a source of stress but a catalyst for engagement, satisfaction, and growth. This may sound counterintuitive, but let's dig a little deeper.

When we speak of accountability, it's not about creating a culture of fear or policing every action of our team members. That's not accountability, that's micromanagement and control. Genuine accountability is about clarity of expectations, open communication, and providing the necessary resources and support for individuals to succeed.

Clarity of expectations means ensuring that every team member understands their role, the goals they are working toward, and the metrics by which their performance will be evaluated. It means fostering an environment where everyone knows not just the 'what' but also the 'why' behind their work. This clarity eliminates ambiguity and provides a roadmap that guides their actions, leading to less stress and more satisfaction.

Open communication involves creating a culture where questions are encouraged, concerns are addressed, and feedback, both positive and constructive, is a regular part of the workflow. In such an environment, accountability becomes an ongoing dialogue that builds trust, reduces anxiety, and fosters a sense of safety and belonging.

Providing resources and support means equipping the team with the tools, training, and assistance they need to excel in their roles. It involves creating a support system that makes them feel valued, seen, and heard. It's about assuring them that it's okay to ask for help and that they are not alone in their journey.

When these elements are in place, accountability doesn't breed stress. Instead, it fuels engagement, satisfaction, and growth. It empowers individuals to take ownership of their roles, all the while knowing they have the information, resources, and support they need to succeed. It creates an environment where employees feel a sense of purpose and commitment, where they are motivated not by fear, but by a desire to contribute to a shared vision.

High accountability should not be a stick to instill fear, but a shared understanding that aligns individual efforts with team goals. It's not about placing blame when things go wrong, but celebrating growth and learning at every step of the journey. It's not about control, but trust.

Embracing this view of accountability requires a shift in mindset. It calls for grit, empathy, and vulnerability. But the rewards are immense. It fosters a culture where everyone knows their role, feels valued, and is empowered to contribute their best. In such a culture, accountability is not a source of stress but a pathway to engagement, growth, and success. As leaders, it's up to us to lead this change and create an environment where accountability is a source of strength, not stress.

Myth 5 -
Accountability means doing things right the first time

A common myth in the discourse of accountability is the belief that it means doing things right the first time. This misconception paints a picture of perfection as the primary goal, and any deviation from this as failure. This outlook not only cultivates a fear-based culture but also misses a fundamental truth about growth and learning. It ignores the reality that mistakes, and the learning derived from them, are invaluable stepping stones on the path to improvement and innovation.

In truth, accountability is not about perfection on the first try. It's about the commitment to continuous learning, improvement, and growth. It's about fostering a culture where making mistakes is seen not as a failure but as an opportunity for learning, innovation, and growth.

Perfection is an impossible standard. When we set perfection as the benchmark, we inadvertently cultivate a fear of failure within our teams. This fear can stifle innovation, limit creativity, and hinder the risk-taking necessary for growth. It can create a culture where individuals are so focused on not making a mistake that they don't dare to venture out of their comfort zones.

On the other hand, when we embrace a culture of learning, we create an environment where individuals feel safe to take risks, and make mistakes, so that they can learn from them. In this culture, accountability is about learning and improving, not about avoiding mistakes at all costs.

As leaders, it's up to us to cultivate this culture. This begins by modeling vulnerability, owning our mistakes, and demonstrating how to learn from them. It means replacing the fear of failure with the courage to learn. It involves shifting the conversation from "What did you do wrong?" to "What did you learn?" You saw this as a prime example when it was time to tell Diane about the charge to Universal for the Harry Potter family. She could have gone directly into discipline, and would have been within her rights as a leader to do so. Instead, she went the route of education, both her learning why I did what I did, and instructing me on what to do in the future.

We must also provide feedback in a way that fosters learning and growth. Feedback should be timely, specific, and focused not only on what went wrong but also on how to improve. It should be delivered with empathy, understanding, and acknowledgment that we are all on a journey of continuous learning.

We must celebrate progress over perfection. Acknowledge that the baby steps of effort and improvement bring us closer to our goals. Accountability fosters a culture where individuals are empowered to take risks, make mistakes, and grow. It's not about doing things right the first time, but about replacing fear with courage, uncertainty with curiosity, and stagnation with innovation.

CHAPTER 9

COACHING, FEEDBACK, DISCIPLINE, OH MY!

Winston Churchill said, "Success is not final, failure is not fatal: it is the courage to continue that counts".[1] This would become my mantra during one of the most difficult times in my professional life. After the amazing experience I had working with Diane and Michele and seeing extraordinary leadership in action, I decided to take a risk and join the World of Disney store as the third shift manager. There had not been a stable third shift manager at that location for some time. As you can imagine, finding someone who wants to work when the rest of the world is asleep is a challenge. I was going to school for my MBA and wanted to try my hand with the big kids. The World of Disney, at the time, was the largest Disney store in the world. You always hear the advice to take risks in your career. You can't have big rewards without big risks. But at that point in my career, I had not experienced failure, and no one had talked about what happens when the risk doesn't pay off. I was about to experience it first hand.

I was at the World of Disney for a very long ten months. I want to be very clear here. I loved the team of Cast Members I worked with. My only true regret during that time was that I was not able to stay with them longer. Together, we had created an unparalleled team that could pull off extraordinary feats. They were the highlight of my time there, and one of the biggest highlights of my time at Walt Disney World as a whole.

The reason why I consider the time at World of Disney a failure though, is because of the leadership. And me. I failed. I knew I was failing. I could feel it and I was being given that feedback. But damned if I couldn't figure out what to do. Have you ever experienced that? Where you know you are failing, and you are fighting with everything in you to do a better job but you just can't figure out how? It happened before in my career, and my leader, Michele, sat me down and we figured it out together. This time was going to be very different. This time there was no coaching, no conversations, no figuring it out together. There was no galvanizing. This time it was me against them. It was a lesson I desperately needed to learn, but it hurt.

I am telling this story because the thing that made this time so different from my previous failure, was the style of leadership utilized. The first time, with Michele, we were a team figuring it out. This time, at World of Disney, I was alone. It was a sink or swim environment, and I was sinking. Many times, as leaders, we feel like we only have one tool we can use when someone is failing. That tool is discipline. But we actually have so many more. Now don't get me wrong, there is absolutely a time and place for discipline, but there is also a time and place for feedback and coaching. We don't only have one tool, and which tool we use will depend on the situation. So let's break down the differences between the three.

Feedback

Many times there are a lot of emotions around feedback. We connect feedback with giving someone difficult or challenging criticism. But it can be positive or constructive. Feedback is the process of giving someone information about a behavior that we either want them to continue doing, in which case it is positive, or we want them to stop doing, which is constructive. There are lots of different ways to offer feedback, and we will discuss a few tactics later.

It is important to note that when you are giving feedback, whether constructive or positive, you are not just talking to the person who is receiving it. You are talking to everything they feel about feedback that they subconsciously bring into the conversation.

Leadership Coach, Consultant and Ph.D. Candidate, John Weng, shared a story about when he was trying to implement change in his organization and was butting heads with one of the department leads. This department was going to receive the biggest benefits, but the lead kept pushing back. In conversations with this individual, John remembers, "We were talking about the service that we were creating, but they were also bringing all of their prior experience of push-back and resistance and lack of trust."

John realized that he was going to have to deal with the underlying issues instead of continuing to focus on the project. If he was unable to get the real problems on the table, they wouldn't be able to move forward. John and his colleague met peer to peer over coffee. John leaned into vulnerability and asked, "What is going on? What is this invisible barrier that we are bumping against and how can we bring it out in the open so we can speak to it?"

Through that open conversation, the colleague shared what was happening, not just in their head, but in their heart, and where all of the push back was coming from, which had nothing to do with John or the current project. With this information, they were able to come up with a solution that would benefit both of them.

When you are having a difficult conversation, you are not only dealing with an individual. You are dealing with all of their complicated emotions around conflict, feedback, expectations, and more. Many times, the invisible undercurrent can be the most destructive to relationships, both personal and professional.

John goes on to say that individuals tend to not be aware of their own invisible undercurrents. They are making decisions due to these undercurrents, such as fear, shame, or problems with authority, but then the individual is rationalizing that decision without being aware of the driver.

Henry Ford famously asked this question, "Why is it everytime I ask for a pair of hands, I get a brain attached?"[2]

We don't work with just hands. We work with the whole individual, including what we see of them and what we do not see. Being aware of that as you move into giving feedback can help remind you to not take it personally if it isn't received well. Do the best you can for the individual in front of you, and then give space for them to react.

Not all feedback is created equally. When a leader sits down to offer someone feedback, there are right and wrong ways to do this. Let's look at what feedback is not.

Feedback is not criticism without action.

Telling someone that they are doing wrong without offering clear and specific steps they can do to improve, is not feedback. When we do this, it creates confusion, frustration, and demoralizes the person you are giving feedback too. Early in my journey with Disney, I was a management intern, and if you know me, you know it is not uncommon for me to be described as intense. At the beginning of my leadership career, intense was an understatement. My leader brought me into his office and let me know he needed to offer me some feedback. Now, I love feedback. I eat it up. Good or bad, tell me how I can be awesome. So when he told me this, I settled in and waited for this tidbit of amazing feedback so I could improve. This is how the conversation went.

Him: Summer, we love what you are doing. The guests love you, the Cast loves you.
Me: Thank you.
Him: We love your passion, we just need you to pull it back a little.
Me: Okay, happy to do that. What does that mean?
Him: Ummmm, how can I put this? We need you to be a little less.....you.
Me: .....

Him: .....

Me: Okay. What does that mean?

As you can imagine, by the end of the conversation, he was frustrated, I was frustrated and neither of us were any closer to getting what we needed from that conversation. All I knew was that I was not doing an amazing job, but I didn't know what to do to fix it.

Feedback is not a good sandwich.

He used what we know as the feedback sandwich. The feedback sandwich was popularized in the 80's by Mary Kay Ash, the founder of Mary Kay cosmetics.[3] When you first hear it, it makes sense:Say something positive, say something constructive, say something positive.

What we now know is that the feedback sandwich doesn't work. People are only going to focus on the positive, and completely lose the constructive. Or, they focus only on the constructive, and don't hear the positive. The use of this tool has also created an environment where we struggle with believing positive feedback. If you are a leader who has used the feedback sandwich, you may have felt a little inauthentic or uncomfortable with the process. These feelings can be translated to the person you are giving feedback to. According to the Harvard Business Review, the feedback sandwich directly undermines the feedback you are giving.[4] When I work with leaders, we discuss this method. I refer to it as the bullshit sandwich. It started with the best of intentions, but we now know that it doesn't have the effect we first thought it would. If you find yourself using it, it is time to retire this particular tool.

Feedback is not judgment or a personal attack.

As we learned in the Manage Yourself First section, our brains like to create stories and make sense of the world around us. This has a lot of benefits, but it can have some drawbacks as well. One of those drawbacks shows up in full force when giving feedback if we are not intentional about it. We turn the feedback into a personal statement where the person receiving the feedback is likely to feel judged or attacked. When we give feedback, we want to focus on behaviors, not *interpretations* of behaviors.

You may recall that we discussed the difference between a behavior and an interpretation a little earlier in this section. For example, you show up for a date and your date has brought you a gift. The behavior in response to this is that you smile. The interpretation made by your date when they see your smile is that you are happy. The interpretation is the story we tell ourselves about what we see happening.

Let's look at it a different way. Imagine you are sitting on a panel for a job interview. After the candidate leaves the room, one of your peers says the candidate was aggressive.

Is "aggressive" a behavior or an interpretation?

It is an interpretation.

What *behavior* did the candidate have that led your peer to believe they were aggressive?

Did they interrupt other candidates?

Did they correct one of the interviewers?

Did they stand extremely close to you on the way out or shake your hand while squeezing to the point of pain, or move your hand up and down rapidly?

These are behaviors that might lead us to the interpretate aggressive behavior.

How about friendly? Is friendly a behavior or interpretation?

That's right! An interpretation.

What *behavior* did the candidate do that led you to believe they were friendly?

Did they smile?

Did they open the door and let someone else in?

Maybe they leaned into the conversation?

Did they nod while you were sharing information?

These are all behaviors that lead us to the interpretation that someone is friendly.

When delivering feedback, we want to think in terms of behavior. Behavior not only helps to avoid feelings of attack and judgment, but it also gives the person actionable steps they can take to improve. For example, if your leader comes to you and says you were rude, it is difficult to immediately know what to do. If your leader comes up to you and says that when they have asked you a question in the past, you interrupt them and start answering the question before they are finished. You know what to do with that information.

Vague comments are not feedback.

Vague comments, such as "great job" or "that could have been better" are not helpful. They show a lack of effort on the part of the leader. When you are preparing to give feedback, whether positive or constructive, put time and thought into it. The person you give the feedback to, will certainly put thought into it. When vague comments are given, they will put an extraordinary amount of thought into what you say because they won't know what to do with the information. Raise your hand if you have had a conversation with someone and went back and thought about it... and thought about it... and thought about it. Put your hand down, the people around you are wondering why you have your hand up.

We want to help others avoid that spiral as much as possible. When giving feedback, you want to be as specific as possible. Many times leaders will avoid giving specific feedback because they don't want to hurt someone's feelings. There is a pervading thought that one can't be kind, *and* direct. These two are not mutually exclusive. Brene' Brown says it best, "Clear is Kind. Unclear is Unkind."[5]

Ignoring the situation, and hoping it will go away, is not feedback.

There are many reasons why we avoid giving feedback. We can rationalize it a hundred different ways. Some of the top reasons are:

1. I don't have enough time.
2. Maybe it will get better on its own.
3. Even if I say something, it is not likely to change.

4. Why say anything? HR will just tell me to do something different.
5. Conflict is bad.

If you have found yourself using any of these reasons, it is okay. We are learning, and as we learn better tools and tactics, we will use them.

When you ignore a situation, it rarely gets better or goes away. Many times, ignoring a situation will have the opposite effect and will cause it to escalate. Imagine you have an employee that is always showing up late for work by five to ten minutes. You don't say anything because you think it isn't that big of a deal. You notice every day that they show up late, and it starts to irritate you. One day, you have to leave on time but you can't leave until you talk to that employee. Your entire day, you know they are going to be late. You grit your teeth, playing the scenario over and over in your head and every time you do, you get a little more frustrated. By the time the employee shows up, you are ready to explode. And you do. The employee is confused and defensive because nothing has been said to them before. So why is it a big deal now?

The relationship is damaged, you are angry, they are angry, and they are probably still going to show up late.

Situation, Behavior, Impact, Intent

The Center for Creative leadership suggests, "The only way to know what someone intended is to ask them - and the only way to let a person know their impact is to tell them."[6]

Early in my career, I was introduced to the, "Situation, Behavior, Impact, and Intent," model from the Center for Creative Leadership. I have been a huge fan of theirs ever since. The SBI model gives leaders a tool that allows them to give feedback that is focused, specific, and objective. It also allows the leader to give feedback that is less personal and more actionable which is a win for both the leader and the person receiving the feedback.

Situation

When you are giving the feedback, you want to help the person understand when and where the situation occurred. You want to be as specific as possible. For example, you might start the feedback with, "When you were delivering your presentation in the manager's meeting on Monday..." This is a very specific time and place. It will help the person receiving the feedback to immediately put themselves back in that moment.

Behavior

When discussing the behavior, as mentioned above, we want to talk through the behavior, not the interpretation of the behavior. You want to keep to the facts. Don't insert your opinion or judgment into this section. Continuing with the example started above, "I asked a question and before I could finish asking it, you interrupted me to give the answer."

Impact

When discussing the impact, you want to talk through the impact of the person's behavior. You want to share the impact from your perspective or a personal perspective.

You want to avoid generalized impacts like "the company lost money." Instead, you want to help them understand the impact to those around them. Because you are describing what you are feeling about what actually happened, the individual is more likely to be able to hear you. From the example above, "The impact on me was that I felt embarrassed and disrespected in front of our colleagues."

Intent

Many times, if you hear the SBI model brought up, it is only discussed with the situation, behavior, and impact. There is another letter that is critically important. Intent is an important part of the conversation. You see, we judge ourselves based on our intent. What did we mean to do? Others judge us on our impact. What did we actually do? When you are giving someone feedback, it is important to not only help them understand their impact, but also to ask about their intent. This helps build trust and keeps the door open for communication. When you are giving feedback, you want it to be a two way conversation, not just you talking at the employee. The completed version of SBI feedback from our original scenario would look something like this:

When you were delivering your presentation in the manager's meeting on Monday, I asked a question and before I could finish asking it, you interrupted me to give the answer. This embarrassed me and I felt disrespected in front of our colleagues. I realize that there may have been more to this than I could see, can you tell me what was going on for you at that moment?

This is a much stronger piece of feedback than, "You were rude to me at the meeting." It also helps to minimize some of the pushback and frustration. "You were rude" opens the door to arguing. "I wasn't rude, you were rude." Whereas, "You interrupted me and spoke over me," is a lot harder to argue with.

The SBI method is also really strong for positive feedback. Instead of giving the feedback, "Great job today," imagine that you said, "Today, as you know, we had three call-ins. You came into work early, took over doing the end of month report without being asked, and were able to complete all of your tasks as well. The impact of this was that I am extraordinarily proud and thankful to have you on my team."

What would be the employee's reaction? As often as you can, start incorporating SBI into your day to day feedback. Focus on the behavior, and make sure it is a behavior, not an interpretation. The more you do it, the smoother the process becomes.

Giving feedback is hard enough. Arm yourself with this tool, and you will find that giving feedback will get easier. It won't get *easy*, but it will get easier.

Coaching

Feedback is about something that has occurred. It is backward looking. Coaching on the other hand is future-facing. Coaching is more about development and growth. It is a long term approach. Coaching is teaching someone how to think through different scenarios and situations, not telling them what to do. When coaching is done well, it helps someone to grow into a better version of themselves. Coaching involves active listening, insightful questions and a healthy dose of empathy and respect. Coaching is not feedback, although feedback may be utilized during the coaching process, and coaching is not discipline. Let's look at what else coaching is not.

Coaching is not giving advice or instructions.

An effective coach is not going to give their coachee the answers. The coach will use techniques such as active listening, questioning, and goal setting to help the coachee move forward. If we use pop culture as an example of effective coaching, think about Yoda. Rarely did Yoda give Luke Skywalker specific direction. Instead, he would ask questions, or tell stories and let Luke connect the dots on his own. Or in more modern times, Ted Lasso. Ted also used coaching techniques to help those on his team grow into better versions of themselves. As leaders, we often go directly to solving the problem for our employees. That is why we were promoted, because we are good at fixing problems. But the reality is that your employees are not broken, so they don't need to be fixed. They are learning and growing, so creating a space for them to do that is critical.

Coaching is not therapy.

Many times, when someone comes to me for leadership coaching the first time, we spend our first session talking through what coaching is, and what it isn't. While a good coaching session can sometimes feel like therapy, it isn't. The easiest way to explain the difference is that coaching looks at the future and therapy looks at the past. While they may intertwine, it will be for a very brief moment. So if you are thinking to yourself that you aren't a therapist, you are correct! You are not. But all great leaders need to be coaches. Not only for their employees, but for themselves as well. One of the most valuable resources a leader has is time, and we never seem to have enough of it. When you utilize coaching skills to help your employees grow, you invest time on the front end, through coaching and guiding them to more effectively make decisions without you, and you get more time on the backend, once they are able to do these things.

Coaching is not micromanaging.

Coaching and micromanaging are direct opposites. Coaching is giving someone the space and time they need to grow, learn, and develop. Micromanaging is overseeing every step a person takes. It is constant critique, and makes the assumption that there is only one right way to do things. When you are coaching someone, you are helping them to figure out *their* way of doing something, not teaching them yours.

Another key difference is that coaching is collaborative. The coach and coachee are on a team together working towards the common goals set by the coachee. Micromanaging is not collaborative, it is telling. The micromanager dictates what is to be done and how. This style eliminates creativity, innovation, and space to be vulnerable.

Discipline

Discipline will generally come after feedback and coaching. There some exceptions to this, which are usually larger violations, such as violence, theft, etc. But for most of our day to day issues as leaders, we will use feedback and coaching first.

You may or may not know, but Walt Disney World is a unionized organization. The majority of the Cast Members I worked with and led were members of a union. Leading in a unionized environment was a special place for new leaders. You either learned fair and consistent practices around discipline, or you became discipline avoidant. I was not going to avoid holding my team accountable, so I had to learn how to ensure that my discipline style was fair and consistent. Thankfully I had Michele when I was learning these lessons.

We had a few Cast Members who were not smiling. I was frustrated with them. They worked at the *happiest place on earth.* Smiling seemed pretty self explanatory to me. I quickly got tired of dropping subtle hints and wanted to go right into writing them up. Yes...I had a lot to learn about leadership. Michele sat me down and asked what was going on and what I was going to do. When I explained, she asked if I had shared with them my expectation that they smile. I looked at her like she had grown three eyes.

"No, I didn't think I needed to tell them to smile."

She then explained the process I would use from then on when dealing with discipline, whether with an employee or with my daughter. Here is the process she shared with me. A note: if you begin this process, from step one, document for yourself the conversation you have and how it went. I do this by sending myself an email so it has a date and time stamp on it. I would also only give four to five days between conversations if the behavior wasn't changing. The purpose of the documentation is if you do move to discipline, you have a written record that you have supplied the employee with everything they need to be able to meet expectations.

This will help if and when you need to get HR involved. The timeline is so that you are not dragging out the process.

1. Never assume that they know what you want them to do. If you have not been very specific in setting the expectation, have the conversation and set the expectation. Using the example from above, that conversation would look something like this:
   a. Hi Cast Member. I wanted to chat real quick about an important part of your job. I have observed over the past few days that when a Guest approaches you, you are not smiling. A smile can seem like a small thing, but Disney expects it from all of us so we can create an open and welcoming atmosphere for our Guests.

2. If you have set the expectation and do not see a change in behavior, bring the employee back in and ask what they need to be able to perform the expectations that were discussed in the prior meeting.
   a. Hi Cast Member, last Wednesday we spoke about the importance of smiling during your shift. I have continued to observe that you are not smiling during your shift. What do you need to be able to do this?
      i. Give them the opportunity to share what they need and then, if it is reasonable, assist them in getting what they need. If you are unable, explain why and see if there is a compromise you can reach with them. Before they leave, ask if they feel they will be able to accomplish the expectation. Inform them that if they are unable to meet the expectation moving forward, the next step will be disciplinary action,

and then explain what that process looks like for your company.

3. If they still do not meet the expectations, bring them in and begin the disciplinary process. Make sure you have looped in HR before this point if your company requires you to do so.

   a. Hi Cast Member. We have been talking about smiling over the past few weeks. We have made the expectation clear and discussed what was necessary for you to be able to meet the expectation. I have observed over the past few days that you are still not smiling. As discussed during our last meeting, this will result in a one point reprimand for a Disney Look violation. Do you have any questions before I have you sign the reprimand?

      i. Now, at this step, sometimes I would get information that would make me rethink delivering the reprimand. Always be open to changing your mind if the information presented makes sense for it. Even at this point, you still want it to be as much of a conversation as possible. The times when I did change my mind and shredded the reprimand, I would let them know this was a one-time thing. If we had the conversation again, it would be a reprimand. They understood and either the behavior changed or the discipline process began.

Discipline is not a bad thing. I want to say it again: Discipline is not a bad thing. If you are being fair, consistent, and educating your employee, but they are refusing to make the change needed, discipline is the logical next step. It is my job as a leader to know the tools available to employees and help them figure out which tool makes the most sense for them. Once we have done that, they have to pick up the tool and begin using it. I can't make the change for them, they have to be willing to do that themselves. If they do not, it is not fair to them or the rest of your team to allow them to do sub-par work. It burns out the other members of your team and undermines your credibility as a leader.

Discipline is not easy, but it is one of the most critical responsibilities of people who choose to lead. No matter the position, the level in the organization, or the individual, do not avoid discipline just because it is uncomfortable for you.

Inspire
YOURSELF & OTHERS

I n March of 2020, I was working my dream job, or at least, what I thought was my dream job.

I was working for an amazing company, geeking out about leadership all day, and when I would get bored, I could leave my office and go down to the floor of the grocery store I supported and interact with employees and customers. It truly was heaven. But if I am being honest, I was starting to flirt with burnout.

I had been in hospitality since I was sixteen. Twenty-two years was a long time. I was getting tired of the long days, missing holidays with my family, and always being on call. The balance was better in this job, but it was still hospitality. To top it off, I was in my car for a minimum of two and a half hours a day due to the commute from a suburb of Dallas, Texas to Plano. Which is why I found my rider losing control of the elephant when my general manager let me know that all salaried leaders would be changing to six days of work a week, on the floor, due to growing concerns around COVID-19. Things got heated very quickly and I found myself leaving the office thinking that everyone was overreacting. After all...it was just the flu.

It is surreal to look back at those times when we had no idea how much everything was about to change. In February of 2020, I gave a keynote speech at a conference in Miami, and was talking to the audience about inspiring themselves. I explained that all of us have a bucket in our bellies. That is the bucket that holds our inspiration (or as I like to say, our pixie dust). When that bucket is overflowing, it is so easy to be inspired and be intentional about inspiring others. But when the bucket is empty, it becomes a lot harder. I didn't talk then about what happens when the bucket disappears.

I honestly didn't know. It was not something I ever had to think about.

But, I was about to find out.

I went from having leadership and employee engagement conversations, helping people with their resumes, teaching leadership classes and generally living my best life, to working six days a week, ten hours a day, on the floor. One morning, shortly after that conversation with my GM, I came into work and it was like a bomb had gone off in the store. We had no product, there were lines wrapped around the store, and we were running on very light staff due to post holiday attrition. I went from focusing on leadership training to helping out in any way that was necessary. For my skill set, that meant working in curbside and the meat market.

All non essential departments found themselves in the same boat as me. Help where we could and try not to get in the way was our motto. The few times when I was in my office, the conversations with employees switched from leadership to more personal concerns. One employee shared that their seventy year old father was in the hospital with COVID and they didn't know if he would make it, and they couldn't go see him. Another said that their spouse, who was the breadwinner, had lost their job, and they weren't sure if they were going to be able to keep their house. Someone else worried about finding child care since their daycare had closed, but needed the job and didn't know how they were going to be able to come in. Another said that English was not their first language, and they were trying to help their 2nd grader manage the online class environment without being able to keep up with what the teacher was saying.

Even now, as I sit on a plane heading to San Diego to spend a week with some of the best leaders in the nation, I find my throat tighten up and my eyes fill with tears at the overwhelming feeling of helplessness that time brings to mind. That was when my bucket completely disappeared. And I couldn't just stop trying to inspire others–they needed it. So I started giving pieces of myself until there was nothing left to give. It was a very dark and angry time for me.

I was angry at how we were showing up as a society, I was angry at how our customers were showing up, I was angry at having to be at work instead of with my family, I was terrified I was going to get my three year old daughter sick, and I was terrified that there was no end in sight. I quickly realized that what had always worked in the past to help me through difficult times was no longer going to work.

I had to do something different. But I wasn't sure what that was going to be.

This chapter is all about finding my "pixie dust," and what the journey helped me uncover. Take what works best for you and discard the rest. This is an extremely personal journey for each of us, and a cookie cutter version simply won't work.

CHAPTER 10

FROM DESPERATION TO INSPIRATION

Why is inspiring yourself important?

The entire landscape of self inspiration has changed since 2020. We have seen what the other side of burnout looks like. We no longer find ourselves getting into bragging contests about the amount of sleep we haven't gotten. We are discovering the value of taking care of ourselves, but we still have many challenges that we have to overcome. Many of us are carrying around old ideas and teachings that are no longer serving us, but we aren't quite sure what to do with them. How do we let go of ideas that shaped who we are at our core?

The short answer...we don't. You can't change who you are overnight. It would be so much easier to rewrite our history so we could step into the future we desire. But that isn't how it works. Instead, we take an intentional step in the direction that we are trying to go, and then we take another, and then another, until we have reshaped our journey into the journey we desire versus the one we accidentally found ourselves on.

We cannot take care of others unless we first take care of ourselves. We have seen this in medical caretakers, including in the skyrocketing rates of burnout with nurses and CNA's, teachers, the way we are rethinking parenting, and so much more. We know what we have been doing is no longer working, but we don't know what to do next.

When talking to leaders and individuals who find themselves responsible for others, they were asked what happens when they continue giving pieces of themselves beyond their natural limitations. 76 percent of them cited resentment as the number one result. You may be familiar with that sensation. Someone asks for something, you say yes, and then when you feel yourself being stretched too thin, you find yourself resenting the person who asked you. But is it their fault?

Sometimes, but most of the time, the responsibility lies in the person who said yes. So how do you know when to say yes and when to say no? Check in with your bucket. Is it full and overflowing? If so, you have more bandwidth to say yes. Is it getting low? Then you need to slow down the yeses. If you find it empty, then you are in triage, meaning you need to be very intentional about what you say yes to and how you are showing up. If you find yourself at this point, it is okay to focus on taking care of you. Once you are beyond burnout and running on empty, it is very difficult to climb out. Ideally, we would want to catch ourselves before we are completely empty, but life doesn't always cooperate. Check in with yourself now and figure out where you are.

Part of my job as a leadership speaker is to travel a lot. I find myself getting confused looks when I mention that I have a young daughter. I used to expect people to ask questions, but I have discovered that instead of asking questions, they make statements, like "It must be so hard to be away from your family," "You must regret having to travel so much," or "How do you stand not being home?" I used to find that I would get defensive when people would make these statements or ask these questions. Now, I roll with it. But people are always surprised by my response. It is normally something like, "My daughter has an incredible support system at home that includes me, my husband and my brother. I am so thankful that we have the setup to allow me to live my life's purpose of reducing the impacts of toxic behaviors in the workplace. And I find that I am able to show up so much better for my family when I am not sacrificing my needs, for what I imagine their needs to be."

This has started many interesting conversations. I can't help but wonder if that question gets asked as often to fathers who travel a lot, but that is for another book. You see, I can't write this book, or stand on a stage, and ask people to take care of themselves so they can show up as the best version of themselves for their family, if I am not also willing to do it.

Is it hard, yes.

Is it worth it? I will tell you in forty years.

Would I change anything? Absolutely not.

This is what it means to inspire yourself. Find what fills your bucket, what brings you joy, and then lean into that. For many of you reading this, it will be your family. For others, it will be volunteer work, or the band you play with on the weekends, or the art you create. All of these things are okay. What is not okay is to continually sacrifice yourself to your loved ones who may or may not want what you are offering them. Too many times we think we know what our loved ones, or our employees, leaders, and/or customers[2] want. And we get mad at them when they aren't "grateful" for everything we are giving them, when they never asked for it.

In 2009, Walmart asked its customers a simple question. Would you like Walmart to be less cluttered? The customers all said yes. Seems like a pretty straightforward question and answer. Then, Walmart began Project Impact. The goal was to remove all of the product in the middle of the aisles and give the retail giant a more open feel. They wanted to attract more high end shoppers and compete head to head with Target. Sounds like a pretty foolproof plan.

By the time they called a halt to Project Impact, Walmart had lost $1.85 billion in sales. This doesn't include the cost of the remodels. OUCH!

This is an undeniable example of what happens when we assume what someone wants. Who is going to answer "no" when asked if they want to shop in a less cluttered store?

While this is on a very large scale, we do this in our day to day as well. For example, we will ask our employees "Do you want more recognition?" When most of them answer yes, we will roll out some giant employee engagement project without asking them why, how often or how they want to be recognized. When they don't respond with gratitude and awe at everything we have done for them, we get emotional. The lower our bucket is filled, the higher the hurt feelings on our part. This is why it is so important to inspire ourselves first.

Inspiring yourself first means always coming back to what is important to you. You don't hurt or neglect your loved ones, but you understand that to show up as the best version of you, for them, means you can't hurt or neglect yourself either.

Myths of inspiring ourselves:

We talked earlier about the myths of accountability. Now we are going to look at the myths of inspiring ourselves. A note about this, as you read through these myths, if you are thinking this doesn't apply to you, read through them anyways. Many of those that you lead or interact with may struggle with these and knowing them, and being able to see the signs in them, can help to have more candid and transparent conversations.

Myth #1 - Focusing on myself is selfish.

This is a myth that shows up time and time again when we start looking at what it means to take care of ourselves. This is due to several sociocultural factors and personal beliefs. Some cultures prioritize taking care of the group over taking care of the self. This is a belief that is many times associated more with traditional stereotypes of women than men. If you are battling with this or know someone who is, recognizing the myth is the first step in being able to determine what is important versus what your mind is telling you is important.

Myth #2 - I will focus on self care when I retire.

In the United States, we have built a culture on productivity and attached our self worth to our ability to produce. I can't tell you how many high achievers I have coached that say they feel intense guilt or anxiety when they are not doing something "productive". Going to the movies can be a source of anxiety for them because the entire time they are watching, they are running their to-do list through their heads. We have learned that we can no longer continue working ourselves into the ground the way we used to. While at Disney, we used to have competitions around sleep. It would go something like this:

Me: I am sooooo tired, I only got six hours of sleep last night
Colleague: Oh, I wish I could get six hours of sleep, I only got two hours of sleep
Other colleague - You got two hours of sleep?! I haven't slept in three weeks!!!

Okay, maybe that is a little bit of an exaggeration, but you get my point. According to the Harvard Business Review, most people operate with a trade off mentality, meaning that if they want to perform better at work, they need to sacrifice something in their personal world to do it.[3] We are seeing again and again that this is not the case. We don't have to spend our entire adult lives giving everything to our work and only then, after we have retired, be able to focus on us. There is a balance to life. That balance is not 50/50. It is what you need it to be, when you need it to be that. And it can change, and should change, based on what you have going on. The goal is to recognize that it is a balance and not a sacrifice.

Myth #3 - I can't move forward until I am inspired.

Inspiration isn't a destination, it is a journey. When we think of the hardest part of any journey, taking the first step is generally at the top. This is why we hear of the diet that never begins, or the degree that we will get some day. Inspiration is the same way. We won't wake up one day and find ourselves inspired. Or at least, we rarely find that happening. Instead, we are intentional and take specific steps to get us closer to what our goal is. When I was working at the grocery store and realized that something had to shift, it would have been so much easier if I could just recognize that I was out of "pixie dust," say I needed more pixie dust and BAM! Have more of it. Instead, I recognized I was out of it, realized all of the ways I normally regenerate weren't accessible at that time, and then got intentional about uncovering different ways to begin the regeneration process. Understanding that you are in need of something is the first step on your journey to recovering it.

Ways to inspire yourself

When I first began my inspiration journey, I remember thinking to myself, "Self, what do people do to recharge?" What I came up with was meditation. So I found a quiet corner, sat myself down criss-cross-applesauce style, and thought to myself, "Okay brain, let's be quiet." Less than a minute later, I was thinking of the person in 3rd grade who had bullied me, and had come up with all kinds of creative and unique ways that I was hoping her life was more difficult than it needed to be.

What I discovered about myself was that meditation is my personal version of hell. There was nothing about it that worked for me, but it led me along a journey of figuring out what *would* work. I am going to offer up a few of those here, but know that your inspiration may look different. Some people exercise, some people play/listen to music, some people use art, some people read, some people spend time with family. There is no right or wrong way for this. You just need to start by asking the questions.

What do you enjoy doing? This question should be answered completely for you. For example, I love playing with slime with my daughter. It is something we both enjoy immensely. Would I play with slime without her, probably not often. So that is not something just for me, but something for us together. When I think of regaining my pixie dust, for me it is reading. I do that by myself, and for myself. So what do you do that is for you? You don't have to do it alone, but it helps if it is something that you enjoy doing with or without others. What do you do that gives you energy? What are those activities that allow your brain to just relax and wander? When you can answer these questions, it is a good starting point. Experiment and explore. As you go on this journey, here are some suggestions to get you started.

Gratitude

The word gratitude comes from the Latin word "gratia," which means grace. It is one of my favorite words, not only for the amazing things it does for us, but also as the reminder to not only have grace for others, but grace for ourselves as well. There is so much research and science that discuss the benefits of gratitude. According to the University of California at Berkeley,[4] there is a very strong connection between gratitude practices and feelings of happiness.

When you practice gratitude, you are teaching your brain to look for moments of joy. Remember from the lesson about our brain and emotional intelligence, our brain is built to find danger, but danger of a specific kind, like a saber tooth tiger. In today's world, we are inundated with "danger". Take for example what we see on the news. It can feel like this is an absolutely terrible time, when in fact, it is one of the safest times in history. Our brain isn't built to handle the safest time in history, which is why it is drawn to danger. While this is natural, it doesn't have to be that way. A simple way to begin rewiring our brain to be able to balance joy along with the precautions it takes to begin a gratitude practice.

The Mayo Clinic suggests the idea of 100 days of gratitude,[5] where you take a picture of something you are grateful for every day. Another way is to write three things you are grateful for, or if you are like me and collect journals instead of writing in them, simply say three things out loud every evening before bed. This begins to teach our brain to look for positivity and joy. This improves health, relationships and so much more.

Include your employees, peers and leaders in this practice. Handwritten thank you notes go a long way, and tend to be cherished keepsakes. Use the SBI feedback model from the, "Galvanize Your Employees," section to give very specific and impactful positive feedback. Help your team understand what you pay attention to, and what good looks like for you.

On a side note, I am grateful for you reading this book. I feel honored and special that you are giving some of our time to read these words. Thank you!

Appreciate Your Body

One of the lessons I am working with my daughter on right now, is to take care of her body, not just in the ways we normally think about, but also in being appreciative of it. Of all the things her body allows her to do, such as receive hugs when she's feeling down, or tickles when she is feeling in a playful mood. Our bodies do amazing things. They allow us to see a beautiful sunset, taste amazing food, and dance for the sheer joy of it. We don't spend enough time showing appreciation to our bodies. If you are anything like me, you have probably spent quite a bit of time pointing out all of the ways your body has let you down.

A key way in finding your inspiration is to spend time being inspired by your body, and also by showing it appreciation. You can show appreciation in a variety or ways. I want to clarify something. This next section isn't to bring guilt or shame, it is to highlight ways that you can be intentional about showing appreciation. If you find yourself experiencing guilt or shame, don't shy away from it, lean into it. Ask yourself where those emotions are coming from. Be curious and ask questions. If you don't know where the emotions are coming from, it can be hard to change the behaviors.

Eating the Right Foods

I love sugar. And not a little, like a lot. I would read about these fad diets, or try some of them, and they would work for a moment or two, and then I would be back to where

I had started. I stopped turning eating into a battleground for my body. Instead of eliminating anything, my family and I focus on moderation. Most of the time I do pretty well in this area. I still have a breakup conversation coming with Diet Dr Pepper, but neither of us are ready to call it quits yet.

Too many times when we think about eating the right foods, we think of living a life of eating salads. This doesn't sound very appealing. Instead of fighting against ourselves for the wrong foods, it can be helpful to start incorporating the right foods when you can. This could be:

- Getting a burger with a salad instead of fries.
- Grabbing an orange instead of a donut at a conference.
- Drinking a glass of water before indulging in sweet tea.

Every good decision is a good decision closer to where you want to be.

Get Moving

Another way to show appreciation to your body is to get moving. It doesn't have to be an hour at the gym. Instead, it can be a quick walk around the block, a dance party with your kids, pets, or partner, channeling your inner ballerina while you are doing chores around the house or parking at the back of the parking lot when you arrive at work.

There are so many ways to get moving that don't include hours in a gym. If the gym is your thing, go after it. If it isn't, get creative. Our bodies do so much better when we move them regularly. We are like the Tin Man from the Wizard of Oz. When we stay in one place too long, we start getting rusty and locking up.

One of my favorite ways to incorporate moving came from a colleague at the Center for Creative Leadership. He recommended "micro breaks" in between meetings. You know those moments we get where we have ten minutes in between meetings? I used to take those moments and break out my phone to lose myself in TikTok. Now, I get up, get moving, fill up my water, and play with my dog. Anything to get out of my chair and away from a screen.

Get Your Checkups

When we think about inspiring ourselves, we normally think about staying away from the doctor, or not going to them. But regular physical, dental, and mental checkups help us stay in tip top shape to be able to handle the day to day struggles that come our way. These checkups are also another way we can show appreciation to our bodies. Consider this your reminder to schedule your checkups.

Sleep

When I was a teenager, anytime I was having an overly emotional moment, my mom would always ask how much sleep I had gotten the night before. This used to infuriate me. My feelings were valid and had nothing to do with my sleep! But it was amazing how much better I felt after I went to sleep. Sleep has the power to help us reset. Sleep helps our ability to make decisions, problem solve and regulate emotions. It improves our memory, ability to manage stress, communicate and can even help to make us more charismatic.[6] It is one of the most important ways we can show appreciation for our bodies, but unfortunately, it is also usually the first thing that gets sacrificed in moments of stress and overwhelm.

There are many ways to inspire yourself. The most important way is to get started. Find small, consistent moments of time to practice self care. You are not trying to completely change your life. Your goal is to gradually fill your bucket and then maintain your bucket. Find what will work for you, *that you will consistently do*, and start there. Add more as it feels right. Onward and Upward!

CHAPTER 11

INSPIRATION ISN'T JUST AN INSIDE JOB

There are so many moments that we interact with another person that seem minor to us, but can change their lives. After my management internship with Walt Disney World ended, I accepted a part time position working at the sports store at Downtown Disney (now known as Disney Springs). I know nothing about sports, which made for some very interesting conversations.

Guest: Do you have a Mickey pin of the Bills?
Me: Is that football...
Guest: ....
Me: Basketball....
Guest: ....
Me: Hockey?
Guest: What are you doing working at a sports store?
Me: I ask myself that every day.

This went on for a few weeks. I wasn't enjoying the job, it was part time and I wasn't getting enough hours and the pay was a huge difference from what I was making as a management intern. I was starting to get frustrated. One day, after a very uncomfortable conversation with a guest about my lack of sports knowledge, I decided I was going to put in notice. As I was walking out that day, my leader, I think her name was Donna, stopped me and said that she knew this wasn't what I wanted, but she appreciated how hard I was working and that it wasn't going unnoticed. She then said goodbye and went on her way. This small moment in time was all it took for me to decide to give it just a little while longer. That was one of the best decisions I have made, because within the month, I was the manager of retail at the Blizzard Beach water park, working for one of the best leaders I have had the privilege of working for, Michele, who you heard about earlier.

It took one moment of my leader's time to completely change my world. Many times, when we think about inspiring others, we think of a huge moment, like Oprah Winfrey giving a car to everyone in her audience, or Steve Jobs rolling out the iPod for the first time. But inspiration isn't these huge moments. Inspiration is made up of hundreds of little moments. Inspiration is consistently showing up for your team.

Remember Duarte from the "Align Your Purpose" section? They have a very unique, and accidental, way of inspiring themselves and others: Giraffes. Giraffes are a permanent, and pervasive part of the Duartian culture, so I had to ask about it when Nancy and I spoke. She shared the story of how one of her employees wanted to create a positive recognition program and asked Nancy if something could be purchased to be passed around in gratitude. Nancy said yes and the employee went out and bought a little statue that was supposed to ward off evil spirits. It was small, angry looking and had beady red eyes. The employee passed the statue to the person she wanted to say thank you to and explained why that statue was chosen. A few hours later, the employee who had received the statue was in Nancy's office, in need of some advice. He loved the concept of the program, but the statue was freaking him out. Nancy advised him to have a conversation with the person who initiated the program, and give her that feedback. She took it to heart and traded the statue in for a giraffe.

Suddenly, Duarte employees were buying giraffes when they went on vacation, or saw them in the stores, and started passing them out for great ideas. Before they knew it, the giraffe was their symbol for inspiration and community.

The giraffe became something much bigger in 2016 when the culture of Duarte was taking a hit. Nancy had been traveling a lot after her Ted Talk, and "wasn't attached to the culture." Nancy recalls, "I [was] in Texas... with an employee and, he is sharing some of the internal struggles happening with the employees, and I was caught by surprise." It felt like a defining moment for her as she remembers asking, "What's a herd of giraffes called? What's it called when giraffes gather?" A herd of giraffes is called a tower. Nancy thought it was exactly what they needed at the moment because, "...a tower is a symbol of refuge and... strength," and her company needed to, " coalesce and be that right now."

I want you to take a moment and think back to the best leader you have ever had. They could have been a mentor, a coach, a manager, or any other kind of leader. This needs to be a person you interacted with regularly, not a sports star or famous CEO. Picture them in your mind, what they did, what they sounded like. Now put a checkmark on all of the behaviors this leader showed:

- ☐ Did what they said they were going to do
- ☐ Made time for you without distractions
- ☐ Truly listened when you spoke
- ☐ Gave you a safe space to share your full self, not just your perfect self
- ☐ Held you accountable when you messed up
- ☐ Didn't make you feel like a failure when you messed up
- ☐ Understood your strengths and taught you how to understand them as well
- ☐ Offered development opportunities
- ☐ Continued to develop themselves
- ☐ Modeled appropriate boundaries (such as not working twenty hours a day, checking emails obsessively, etc.)
- ☐ Taught you how to solve your own problems vs. solving them for you

The list above is what individuals I have spoken to consistently say when asked why a leader inspires them. You don't see huge things on here. These are small, consistent steps that leaders take to motivate, inspire, and build trust with their teams.

When you consider inspiring your teams, don't get overwhelmed thinking you have to do something huge. Show up, make sure they understand their value, help them grow and become better, tell them the truth, both constructive and positive, and be the leader they need you to be.

That is what inspiring others is.

Where do our employees fall in terms of needs?

Maslow's Updated Hierarchy of Needs[1]

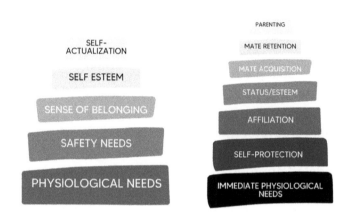

You may have heard of Maslow's hierarchy of needs. In his original work, Maslow stated that our order of needs exists in a hierarchical model. The first being physiological needs such as food, water, and shelter. Then you move to safety all the way to self-actualization.

This work has been reviewed and there have been some questions raised about how accurate it truly is. A group of scientists decided to take another look and came up with a modified version.[1] In this, self-actualization was removed completely and the five-level-pyramid went to seven levels. The point is, every person's needs are different, and what we previously defined as 'self-actualization,' may be different from person to person. Melissa Adams, Executive Vice President of HR for Duarte, sums it up nicely, "If you don't

get the basic stuff right, you cannot expect people to innovate and be creative and solve big hairy problems for your
clients."[2]

You may be wondering why we are covering stuff you
learned in Psychology 101. It is because if you are trying to
lead others, you need to understand that their needs and
your needs may not align. For example, a general manager in
the restaurant industry may be making close to, or over, six
figures. Chances are, their front line employees are barely
making minimum wage, are living paycheck to paycheck,
and struggle to pay all of their bills. The general manager
may be more financially stable, so their needs are going to
look different.

Another example may be a leader who works with a lot of
college interns and new graduates. That leader's employees
may be focused on finding a mate, whereas the leader may
be happily married and settled.

The needs of your employees are not any less important
than your needs, but recognizing the differences is critical to being able to inspire, motivate, and understand what
drives them.

Intrinsic versus extrinsic motivation

Another area of importance when understanding your
employees is intrinsic vs. extrinsic motivation. Central to
this understanding is the distinction between intrinsic and
extrinsic motivation, two powerful forces that can shape
the way people work, interact, and ultimately contribute to
the success of an organization.

Intrinsic motivation comes from within an individual. It is a drive that arises from the pleasure and satisfaction that a person finds in the activity itself. It's the desire to engage in a task because it is inherently enjoyable or fulfilling. Imagine a software engineer who gets lost in coding, not because they're eyeing a promotion, but because they love the thrill of solving complex problems, or a customer service representative who goes the extra mile for clients because they genuinely enjoy helping people and resolving issues. These are examples of intrinsic motivation.

Extrinsic motivation, on the other hand, originates from factors external to the individual. It is driven by the promise of a reward or the fear of punishment. Extrinsic motivators include salaries, promotions, benefits, recognition, or penalties like job loss or reprimands. These are the tangible and intangible rewards that organizations often use to encourage productivity and performance.

Both forms of motivation have their place, and can be useful in different circumstances. However, when it comes to fostering long-term engagement, creativity, and resilience in the face of challenges, all of which are integral to the success of any organization, intrinsic motivation generally holds the edge.

Why is that the case? The key is authenticity and a sense of purpose, which are at the heart of intrinsic motivation. When employees feel intrinsically motivated, they are operating from a place of authenticity. They are engaging with the work because it aligns with their personal values and interests, not merely because they are pursuing an external reward or avoiding a penalty. This level of authenticity leads to deeper engagement, more creative problem-solving, and a greater willingness to take risks and embrace challenges.

After I graduated with my bachelor's, I had the opportunity to work for CITGO Petroleum on an internal auditor internship. I was making BANK! I went into that job thinking I was going to be an internal auditor when I grew up. It took less than a week before I realized that money isn't everything, and there wasn't enough money in the world to keep me in this job. This is not to say anything against those that do auditing, we need you and your skill set, and appreciate what you do. But it was not my skill set. I found it extremely demotivating and difficult.

Fast forward, I left that well paying job and went to work at Disney, making almost 75 percent less. And stayed there for almost ten years. This is why it is important to understand your values, interests, and skills as well as those of your employees.

Moreover, intrinsic motivation tends to support a sense of purpose, which we discussed in the, "Align Your Purpose," section. Employees who are driven by intrinsic motivation are likely to feel a deeper connection with the broader mission of the organization. They see the impact of their work, feel a sense of pride in their contributions, and are motivated to continue giving their best.

In contrast, while extrinsic motivation can be effective in achieving specific, short-term goals, it may not be as effective for promoting long-term commitment and innovative thinking. Relying heavily on extrinsic motivators can sometimes lead to a 'carrot and stick' culture that stifles creativity, discourages risk-taking, and leads to burnout.

This is not to say that extrinsic motivators are irrelevant. Salaries, benefits, and recognition are important. They can attract talent and signal appreciation. But they are often not sufficient. Individuals also crave a sense of belonging and purpose, opportunities for growth and learning, and the autonomy to make meaningful decisions.

The key is to strike a balance and recognize that employees are not simply driven by rewards or penalties, but also by a desire for fulfillment, growth, and purpose. It is about fostering an environment where employees feel valued, connected, and motivated to bring their whole selves to work.

The Care Model

Just as our employees have natural strengths, we have natural strengths as well. Some leaders will be excellent at the inspirational piece and will be naturally motivating. Others will not. If you find yourself in the first category, this is a tool that can enhance what you are already doing well. If you are in the second category, this tool can help you be intentional about your employees and their needs. It may not feel natural, but if you are doing it for the right reasons, it will not be inauthentic. Your employees will appreciate your focus and intention on learning how to lead them individually and more effectively.

Community

As we discussed earlier in this chapter, your employees want to feel like they are a part of something bigger than themselves. A truly eye-opening moment for me during the pandemic was when I was talking to my husband, Miles. He had been working from home for the first time. I assumed it would be heaven for him. You see, my husband is an introvert. If he could never speak to anyone other than myself and our daughter, I think he would be okay with that. So I assumed that working from home would allow him to completely introvert, focus on his tasks, and he would be super energized. And he was... for the first few months. But then I started noticing that he was getting a little irritable and when he talked about work it sounded like there was a hint of anger in his words. I was confused and dug in a little deeper. He told me that he missed being at work. He wanted to be back in the office where he was surrounded by people, even if they left him alone. He was missing the community of the workplace.

When we think of organizations with amazing cultures, one of the top comments by employees is that they feel like they are a part of something bigger than themselves. This was how we felt at Disney. It meant something to be a cast member. I get asked all of the time if I miss it, and every time, I answer with a passionate yes. The thing I miss the most was being a cast member. There was so much pride in those two words. Even today, almost six years after leaving Disney, I am on vacation with my family and wearing a Mickey Mouse pride hat. Someone commented on it and how much they love Disney, and when I said I had worked there, they lit up and started asking tons of questions. Their reaction brought back all of the pride and nostalgia of what it means to be a cast member. Never underestimate giving your team something bigger than themselves. We have seen this in business and in sports. Individuals coming together to be bigger than themselves. We cheer for it in our movies such as *Saving Private Ryan* or *Remember the Titans*, we cry while reading the books such as *Harry Potter* or *Moneyball*, and we know it when it happens to us in the workplace.

Authenticity

The goal with authenticity is to allow your employees to show up as their authentic selves. People feel valued when they can be their full selves, not just the cookie cutter version of whatever their organization feels is the ideal. Creating a safe environment for individuals feels like a lot of work but it is absolutely the responsibility of the leader.

I want to be very clear here, authenticity does not give someone the right to be an asshole. It does not excuse bad behavior. It drives me batty when someone does something they know is in bad form and immediately excuses it with, "I am just being honest" or, "You wanted me to be authentic." Being authentic means allowing a space for everyone to show up as their authentic self, within the boundaries of the team.

Remember when we spoke of authenticity as shades of color, where I was a deep purple? This is one of the times where you can adjust the color to the needs of the group without being inauthentic. I can be intense, and that intensity has its time and place, but it isn't every time, and every place. By imagining that my fullest, most intense self is the royal purple, when I go into a meeting with someone where I need to listen, I visualize in my head toning down my color to a violet. On the other hand, you may be more of a violet, or someone who observes, listens a lot, and doesn't chip in or share ideas freely. If you are invited to a brainstorming meeting where your ideas will be important and things are moving quickly, you may need to turn your purple up to a darker purple. You are still you, you have your dreams, motivations, and values, and you are not having to sacrifice any of those. You are simply adjusting to the needs of the team.

This is important for your team as well. You need to give them space to try new things without fear of being made fun of or called out if they make a mistake. They should be able to talk about their lives outside of work in a way that is received and appreciated. This is what it means when we talk about authenticity.

Relevance

Fyodor Dostoyesvky, a Russian author from the 1800's, is quoted as saying, "If one wanted to crush and destroy a man entirely, to mete out to him the most terrible punishment... all one would have to do would be to make him do work that was completely and utterly devoid of usefulness and meaning."

This concept was tested by making prisoners of war dig and refill the same hole over and over again. It was considered an effective form of torture due to the psychological impact it had on the prisoners.[3]

In today's professional world, our employees are doing tasks because they were assigned it, but they don't understand the why behind it. These tasks become menial, boring, and to the employee, meaningless. Spending time helping your employees understand the importance of why they do what they do is critical when helping them find their "pixie dust." We discussed this at length in the "Align Your Purpose" section of the book, but we want to spend just a moment here as well. Many times, relevance is a huge factor in how an employee feels about their job. We have seen the impact of this when we were customers. Imagine the best server you have had, or the amazing front desk employee who checked you in, or that work colleague who is always chipper, no matter what. These are people who have found their relevance in what they do.

One of my favorite parables is about the bricklayers. After the great fire of 1666 that tore through London, Christopher Wren was commissioned to rebuild St. Paul's Cathedral. He observed three bricklayers, two of which were half standing and working at a moderate pace. The third was standing tall and working very quickly. Wren approached the bricklayers and asked him what they were doing. The first responded with, "I am a bricklayer. I am laying bricks to feed my family." The second replied with, "I am a builder, I am building a wall," and the bricklayer said, "I am building a great cathedral to the Almighty." All three had the same job, but the relevance that they found within the job was different. None of their reasons for doing the job was wrong, but the third bricklayer was doing the job for something greater than himself, and it showed in how he worked.

When you consider your job and your team's, what is the relevance behind what you do? If you are in accounting, you handle the money. You ensure that the business has the money it needs to be able to make an impact on the world. If you are in payroll, you don't just process checks, you ensure that employees have the ability to take care of their families. Dig into why you do what you do and why it matters. When you can answer that question, it makes filling your bucket easier. It may not get easy, but it will get easier.

Empowerment

The final piece of the "Care" model is empowerment. When you have created an environment that, "galvanizes your employees," you have individuals that have boundaries, and know what needs to get done, and how they factor into the responsibilities of the team. Once that happens, you get the fun of watching them blossom. To do this, a leader has to be intentional about creating an environment of empowerment. This is done through coaching and guiding your employees to be able to solve their own problems versus having to come to you to solve the problem. This will look different depending on the employee, their experience, etc. You will empower an intern differently than you will empower someone who has ten years of experience. Being intentional, looking for moments of empowerment, and times you can help your employees grow to the next level is the goal.

When I transitioned to H-E-B, there was a leader known for saying that their job was to get their team to the point that they no longer needed them. This was terrifying to me. If I wasn't needed by my team, would I get fired?! What was this nonsense? So I asked. He explained that when a leader can get their team to the point where the leader is no longer needed, the leader will have more time to start working more strategically and at a higher level. They will also have created a team that has a natural succession plan so when the leader is ready to be promoted, it wouldn't be a source of discomfort trying to determine who was going to fill the leader's position. In short, when the leader got their team to a point where they were no longer needed, the leader would find themselves promoted shortly after. And he was right. Once I got out of my own way and started building a team that could function without me, I was promoted.

During this process, I discovered a powerful question for empowerment. When an employee would come to me and ask what they should do for a situation, I would respond with, "If I wasn't here, what would you do?" This allowed the employee to begin thinking through the situation within a safe environment, but in a way that allowed them to begin the step toward empowerment.

Leadership By Coffee

We heard from Tyrone Frost, retired Air Force and current major airline pilot, earlier in the "Align Your Purpose" section. I met him during one of my flights. He happened to be sitting next to me and I noticed his badge. When I realized he was a pilot, I got ridiculously excited and asked if he wanted to be interviewed for my book. He obviously thought I was a little off my rocker, but continued chatting with me. When we landed, I asked for his name and told him I would follow up. I can imagine his surprise when I reached out to him via LinkedIn and asked for dates that would work for the interview. Thankfully he agreed and during our interview, he mentioned something that he called "Leadership by Coffee," which was such a simple description for a profound leadership style.

It immediately made me think of Megan, my general manager when I worked at the grocery store. She led our store during COVID-19, and it was an interesting experience watching leadership happen on such a large scale. She had my loyalty before, and after, the pandemic. I would have done just about anything for her. But she is the picture of "Leadership by Coffee." Every morning, she would go to the coffee bar, order her coffee, talk to the employees and guests while fixing her coffee, and then walk the floor of the store talking to everyone she passed. Unless something major was going on, she wasn't offering a lot of direction, she was taking a pulse of the people and the store. Every employee knew her by name and looked forward to her walking the floor in the morning. The front line leaders all knew her, knew her expectations and took pride when she would stop and ask how they were doing, asked about their family, and asked about things they were proud of in the store. Every morning started this way for the multiple years we worked together. She took a store that was not hitting its budgets and within a few years turned us into the store that was held up as the model. The morale was high, the performance was high, and we weathered any storm, or pandemic, thrown at us.

All of this was done via "Leadership by Coffee." Don't underestimate being intentional about spending time with your team. If you are in a virtual world, create morning coffee as an open zoom meeting that people can pop in and out of to say hi. Drop meetings on your team's calendar just to spend ten minutes catching up and checking on them. The key isn't to create the perfect moment, it is to be intentional about opening up time to have hundreds of imperfect moments. The imperfect moments are where the inspiration happens.

CHAPTER 12

THE ENGAGEMENT VS. MORALE DILEMMA

What if what we know about employee engagement is wrong? Often, our understanding of engagement and morale is reduced to oversimplified notions like, engaged employees are those willing to go the extra mile, and high morale equates to a happy and content team. But beneath these generalized concepts are deeper, more nuanced realities that deserve our attention and understanding.

Engagement is not merely an employee's willingness to invest additional effort and time into their work; it is their psychological investment, their connection to their work, and the alignment of their values and purpose with the organization's mission. An engaged employee does not just perform tasks but is passionate about their contributions and feels a profound connection to their work and the organization.

However, it's essential to acknowledge that engagement cannot be controlled or demanded— it can only be cultivated. Leaders must facilitate an environment that empowers employees to be their authentic selves, where they can express their ideas without fear and find resonance between their personal values and their work. In such an environment, engagement naturally blossoms.

On the other hand, morale embodies the collective mood and attitudes of employees towards their work environment, their peers, and the organization at large. High morale often manifests as a positive and optimistic work environment, characterized by mutual respect, strong team cohesion, and a shared sense of purpose. While it's tempting to equate high morale with an always-cheerful team, this perception is misleading.

Morale, in reality, is about fostering a resilient and supportive work culture where employees feel safe enough to express their concerns and challenges, and where these concerns are addressed, not dismissed. It's about being seen and heard. High morale isn't about the absence of problems or conflict, but the presence of empathy, understanding, and constructive problem-solving.

Understanding the profound dynamics of engagement and morale requires challenging our conventional wisdom. It requires us to look beyond the surface and explore the depths of these constructs and their impact on organizational health. When we see things such as an employee engagement survey, understand that the survey is a tool that allows us to know what is going on with our teams on a deeper level, but it is not the golden ticket that many organizations feel it is.

As leaders, it's time to shun the comfort of oversimplified perceptions. It's time to acknowledge the complexities of engagement and morale, to understand their interconnectedness, their roots, and their impact. By doing so, we can cultivate workplaces where employees are not just physically present, but emotionally and psychologically invested, where they feel seen, heard, and valued, resulting in not just higher productivity and retention, but a more fulfilling work experience.

The Connection between Happiness and Engagement

Many times, when I am coaching a new leader, they will come to me with frustration around team morale. They will say that morale is low and they don't know what to do. I typically ask about accountability when this happens. They often look confused and say they need to know about morale, not about accountability. But these two pieces are connected in a very strong, but sometimes invisible way. One of the unintended consequences of focusing so heavily on engagement without fully understanding it, is that leaders think they have to make their employees happy. Decades of research into happiness has uncovered some surprising results. Happiness has more to do with the individual than we originally thought.

According to the self-determination theory,[1] autonomy (the need to direct one's own life) and mastery (the desire to learn and improve) are two essential elements of happiness and engagement. When individuals feel they have control over their tasks and see opportunities for personal growth, they are more likely to be happy and engaged.

Can leaders influence this? Absolutely! Are leaders responsible for this? No. Understanding what energizes and inspires your employees is critical to effective leadership. You want your employees to follow you by choice, not because they feel they have to. But you will build trust and respect from them by creating a safe environment where they feel like they have autonomy and mastery. A leader creates the environment that allows these to grow or extinguish and the employees do the rest.

The Illusion of Control

We need to have a chat. I am going to share with you something you may not like. I apologize in advance, but it is a critical piece of information for leaders to not only know, but to believe in their hearts and minds. *We have no control over our employees.* In fact, the only thing we can control is ourselves.

We live in a world that is obsessed with control, especially in the corporate world. Leaders often feel an intense need to control outcomes, processes, and people. We discussed earlier how this need to control showed up in force when so many jobs were switched to a work-from-home format in 2020. All of a sudden there was a flood in software tools that tracked employees' performance. It tracked mouse clicks, time in between computer tasks, etc. Tell me a company doesn't trust their employees without telling me a company doesn't trust their employees... Hint: it's one that uses this software.

Control is an illusion. This truth is as applicable to the concept of employee engagement as it is to any other aspect of life or work.

Employee engagement is a deeply personal, individual experience. It involves one's emotional investment and commitment to their work and the organization. Contrary to the belief that leaders can 'manage' engagement, the truth is that they can not. What they can do, however, is create an environment where engagement can naturally flourish.

Often, leaders mistake compliance for engagement. Employees might comply due to fear, the need for job security, or the desire for promotion, but that is not engagement. True engagement comes from a place of genuine commitment, passion, and alignment of personal values with the organization's goals. It can't be dictated or managed from the top. Instead, it is nurtured from within each individual.

This realization calls for a significant shift in our leadership approach, from one of control to one of empowerment.

Empowering Autonomy

As leaders, the best we can do to cultivate engagement is to empower our employees with the autonomy they need to explore, innovate, and express their authenticity at work. We need to trust our employees by providing them the space to unleash their potential and contribute in the most meaningful ways they can.

Empowering autonomy isn't about relinquishing leadership. Instead, it's about leading from a place of *trust and respect*, and acknowledging the competence and capabilities of our team members. It's about setting clear expectations, providing necessary resources, and stepping back to let our employees take the driver's seat in their roles.

If you are finding yourself having a strong response to what you are reading, maybe you are getting defensive or are expressing doubt, I want you to spend a moment with those feelings. Where are they coming from? What have you been taught or shown that leads you to believe that employees are inherently not to be trusted? Many of us have been taught this way and we are working to overcome it. If you find yourself responding strongly, don't fight it, listen to it, be curious about it, and lean into it to uncover where it is coming from. Until you know its source, it can be hard to work through it.

When employees are given autonomy, they feel valued, trusted, and respected. They experience a heightened sense of ownership and accountability for their work. This sense of autonomy is a powerful motivator, sparking passion, inspiration, commitment, and hence, engagement.

At this point, you might be asking, "How do we, as leaders, empower autonomy?" The answer lies in fostering open communication, encouraging initiative, appreciating diverse perspectives, supporting skill development, and accepting that mistakes are part of the learning process.

Inspiring Engagement Through Authentic Leadership

Leading by example is another crucial aspect of fostering engagement. As leaders, our actions, attitudes, and behaviors set the tone for our teams. When we demonstrate passion, commitment, and authenticity in our roles, we inspire the same in our team members.

Authentic leadership is about being true to who we are, and leading with our hearts as well as our minds. It's about embracing our vulnerabilities, acknowledging that we don't have all the answers, and being open to learning from others, including those we lead. Remember the example we used earlier about purple and adjusting the shade? This connects here as well.

Authentic leaders recognize the strengths of their team members and enable them to leverage their talents optimally. They encourage a culture of open and honest communication where everyone feels safe to express their ideas, opinions, and concerns. This creates an atmosphere of trust and mutual respect, which serves as a fertile ground for engagement to thrive.

Inspiring engagement through authentic leadership also involves recognizing and appreciating our team members' efforts and contributions. Recognition affirms their value and significance in the organization, which in turn fosters a deeper sense of commitment and engagement.

In conclusion, it's time we debunked the myth of managed engagement and embraced a new understanding of leadership, one that empowers autonomy and leads by example. When we let go of the illusion of control, we allow ourselves to lead from a place of authenticity, vulnerability, and empathy.

Remember, as leaders, our job isn't to manufacture engagement. It's to create an environment that invites it. This involves shifting our leadership paradigms, relinquishing control, and leading with authenticity. Because at the end of the day, it's not about being in control, but about being connected— connected to our authentic selves, connected to our team members, and connected to our shared purpose.

This is all great...but how do you actually do it?

We have talked about engagement, morale, happiness and more. We know that leaders can influence the environment to create a space that invites higher levels of engagement and morale. But how do we turn these concepts into real, tangible results in our organizations? How do we create a work environment that invites, nurtures, and sustains engagement?

Creating an engaging environment isn't about installing fancy perks or giving motivational speeches. Instead, it is about creating a space where people feel safe to be themselves, where they feel seen, heard, and valued. It's about fostering a culture of trust, respect, and connectedness. Here are some practical techniques to nurture such an environment.

Foster Psychological Safety

We heard about Google's Project Aristotle[2] earlier. This project found that the number one factor that distinguishes successful teams is psychological safety. This refers to an environment where people feel safe to take risks, make mistakes, and voice their thoughts without fear of ridicule or punishment. Yes we talked about it before, but it bears repeating. As leaders, we can cultivate psychological safety by encouraging open communication, acknowledging our own mistakes, and handling failures as learning opportunities.

Empower with Autonomy

As we've discussed earlier, empowering autonomy is crucial for fostering engagement. It's about trusting our team members with the freedom to express their skills, ideas, and initiative. When we set clear expectations, provide resources, and allow our employees to manage their tasks, we are showing them that we trust their judgment and abilities.

Establish Clear and Meaningful Goals

People are more engaged when they have clear, meaningful goals that align with their personal values and the organization's mission. As leaders, we must ensure that our team members understand how their work contributes to the larger purpose. This sense of purpose infuses their work with meaning and spurs engagement.

Promote Learning and Development

A culture that values learning and development is fertile ground for engagement. When we encourage and provide opportunities for continuous learning, we send a message to our team members that we value their growth and are invested in their future. This not only boosts their skills, but also their engagement.

Appreciate and Recognize

Recognition is a powerful motivator. Regularly acknowledging and appreciating the efforts, achievements, and contributions of our team members makes them feel valued and seen. It affirms their significance in the organization and deepens their connection and commitment to their work. Skip out on the generic, "Thank you," and go back to the SBI model from the "Galvanize Your Employees" section. Make it specific, relate it to the behavior and discuss the impact it had on you. This technique is so much more powerful than the generic statements we tend to make.

Cultivate Relationships

The quality of relationships in the workplace significantly influences engagement. Building strong, respectful relationships based on trust and empathy makes people feel connected and part of a community. This involves fostering a culture of collaboration, inclusion, and mutual support.

These are just a few techniques to create an engaging environment. Each organization, each team, and each individual is unique, and thus, there is no one-size-fits-all approach. It requires intention and courage to venture into this unknown to be able to tailor these techniques to the unique needs and circumstances of our teams.

Remember, this isn't a one time task. It's a continuous journey, and a commitment to creating a space where people can bring their whole selves to work. As leaders, our role is not to dictate or control, but to serve as courageous gardeners, planting the seeds of engagement, watering them with trust and respect, and allowing them to blossom in their own unique ways. This is how we inspire— hundreds of little steps, consistently taken.

Control
YOUR CHAOS

t is the summer of 2020, the pandemic is in full force, arguments over masks have escalated, and people are showing up in ways that are surprising. Tensions are high after the George Floyd and Brianna Taylor murders. I am working in the grocery store and it is absolutely nuts. My job had shifted from working in the meat market and curbside departments to being the manager on duty at Protein Alley.

This is Protein Alley, named because there is an old style butcher shop on the left side and the longest seafood counter in Dallas on the right side. This was my view for ten hours a day. Before COVID, we could fit one hundred people, shoulder to shoulder, in this space while they waited on their meat and seafood products. And it was worth the wait, the products are phenomenal.

Post COVID, we could have twelve people in that space before things started getting too tight. We assumed our community would have our back and make the changes with us. They had always had our backs before. This time was different. They were scared, they were angry, and they were overwhelmed with change. So when they went to the grocery store and experienced more change, they lashed out. It got to the point that a leader had to be in this space from store open, to store close, to handle all of the emotions that the customers were throwing our way. We had armed guards walking the stores, so customers could see them and know they were there. These weren't your regular rent-a-cops. These were previous military men and women who you absolutely did not want to mess with. They hung out a lot with us in Protein Alley, an extra measure to keep people from escalating too much.

This was what we were dealing with day in and day out.

If you worked in person during the pandemic, you probably had your own version of the COVID dance. My COVID dance was that when I would get home, I would take off my shoes and my outer layer of clothes. Then I would race through the house to jump in the shower with one thought, "Please don't let me get my family sick."

One night, I got home late. It had been a wild few weeks. I had not seen my daughter other than in passing for what felt like weeks. When I walked in, all of the lights were out. I wanted a moment, just a moment, to just be. I walked in, sat on the couch and leaned my head back. Eyes closed, I let my mind wander and worked on bringing the adrenaline and anxiety down to manageable levels. I heard a door opened and assumed it was Miles coming out to say hello. When I opened my eyes and raised my head, I realized it was my beautiful three year old daughter that I was terrified of getting sick. She raced over to me, a huge smile on her face and open arms, and all I could think of was, "Don't let her touch you." I put my hands on her shoulders, pushed her back and loudly said "No!" I watched those beautiful brown eyes fill up with tears and felt like the world had slammed down on top of me. I knew at that moment that I couldn't keep doing what I was doing. It wasn't working and I felt like I was being pulled apart.

I had heard a question many years earlier, before I was a wife and mother, that I didn't really understand. At that moment, that question played loudly and repeatedly in my head.

Is your family getting the best of you, or the rest of you?

They weren't even getting the rest of me— there wasn't anything left. These moments in time, the one you read about in "Inspire Yourself First," and this one, were pivotal moments for me to begin rethinking what I wanted in life. I became intentional about asking myself if I wanted something because I *thought* I should want it, like a cushy corporate gig, or if I wanted something because I *actually* wanted it. This was the first step of many in "Controlling My Chaos."

CHAPTER 13

MAXIMIZING YOUR MOMENTS - TIME MANAGEMENT VS. ENERGY MANAGEMENT

When I was an intern, we switched leaders a little over halfway through my six month program. I was determined to get a full time leadership position at the end of my internship, so I was doing everything I thought a good leader did. I showed up early, stayed late, and took on every project.

One evening, after having been at work for a little over eleven hours, my leader walked by on her way home and commented on how long I had been working. I puffed up with pride that she noticed and told her I had a few more things to do and then I would be heading out. She then looked at me with a very serious expression and told me that my job, as it had been created, should be able to be done in nine hours. If I was still here after eleven hours and I wasn't done yet, either I was bad at managing my time or I was trying to make a point that didn't need to be made.

That was not the response I was expecting. Instead of getting kudos for working late, I was chastised. She then said something I would never forget, "You have the exact same amount of hours in your day as anyone else. You have twenty-four hours, just like Mark Zuckerberg, Walt Disney, and Queen Elizabeth. If you can't figure out how to best manage them, you will end up wasting time you will never get back."

This immediately caused me to look at time differently. But it would take a pandemic before I would make specific changes to begin "Controlling My Chaos." You see, to control your chaos, you have to look at more than just time, you also have to consider your energy.

Time Management vs. Energy Management

The only thing I knew about energy was that sometimes I had it and sometimes I didn't. When I had it, it was amazing! When I didn't, it sucked. But it was not something I was ever intentional about. Growing up working in hospitality, there wasn't a whole lot of conversation around balance and wellness. You did the job that needed to be done or you didn't make it. Coping mechanisms were created that worked for the normal stuff, but when there wasn't any normal left, the coping mechanisms stopped working. I went from being burned out to being straight up crispy. Something had to give.

The first thing that had to give was how I viewed energy management. In the United States, we value productivity above all else. As discussed in the, "Inspire," section, working hard was seen as a requirement, not a suggestion. And working until the job was done was critical if you wanted to succeed. Things like meditation, or self care were seen as selfish or something for hippies. I had a lot of guilt and shame around saying, "I can't do this, I am not okay." It was as though I was letting everyone down by admitting that I was human. I still have a certain amount of guilt and shame, but I heard someone say something that put it into perspective, which was that guilt is a small price to pay for happiness. And they were so right.

Time Management

In the realm of time management, it's vital to understand what it is and, importantly, what it is *not*. Let's start with what time management is not. Time management, at its essence, isn't merely the mechanics of scheduling, setting deadlines, or the ticking away of seconds, minutes, and hours. It isn't obeying an unforgiving schedule, nor is it the measure of our worth by the number of items crossed off a to-do list. It is not removing all hints of downtime, nor is it a sacrifice to the productivity gods. Time management is not about perfection, or the unattainable goal of fitting twenty-five hours into a twenty-four-hour day.

Contrary to popular belief, time management is not a direct connection to success. You could manage your time flawlessly, fitting your responsibilities and obligations into neatly scheduled blocks, and still feel dissatisfied. This is because time management is not about squeezing as much as we can into our days. It's not a weapon to wield against pro-crastination or an antidote to disorganization.

Now, let's illuminate what time management is. Time man-agement *is* a tool to be utilized in the way that makes most sense to you and your needs. Time management is aware-ness about how we spend our time and an alignment of our actions with our values. It's an act of setting boundaries around our time so that we can engage in activities that nourish us physically, mentally, and emotionally.

Time management is also a courageous act. It requires the courage to say no, the courage to set boundaries, the cour-age to prioritize, and above all, the courage to choose. It's an exercise in admitting that we are not superheroes and that we cannot do everything. It's an acceptance that we are imperfect humans and we move through this world better when we do it with others. It is when we are able to ask for, and receive assistance instead of only relying on ourselves.

At its core, time management is about engaging whole-heartedly and intentionally with our lives. It's the intentional choice to spend our time on activities that align with our values, goals, and dreams, and that fill us with a sense of purpose. It's the willingness to step back from the tyranny of the reactive, and instead focus on the proactive.

Importantly, time management is a tool that enables us to live our lives with intention and choice. It is a form of self-respect that allows us to value our time and the pur-suits we choose to undertake. It provides a framework for us to be intentional, mindful, and purposeful with our time. This intentional approach prevents us from falling into the trap of being *busy*, a state which can disconnect us from our sense of self and from those who matter most.

In this paradigm shift, we need to remember that time is not something to be controlled, but something to be respected. Time is our most valuable non-renewable resource. Thus, managing time is not about control, but about respect, authenticity, and the intentional choice to engage with our lives.

Energy Management

Just as we dived into the labyrinth of time management, let's unravel another critical aspect of our lives: energy management. A concept deeply intertwined with our human capacities, energy management can seem like tricky terrain to navigate, particularly in a world that often equates busyness with worthiness.

To engage with this concept meaningfully, let's first explore what energy management is not. Energy management is not about pushing yourself to the brink of exhaustion to squeeze productivity from every waking moment. It is not a pursuit to keep your energy levels at a peak at all times, nor is it about denying yourself rest when you need it. It isn't the relentless filling of your day with tasks, meetings, and chores in an attempt to prove your worthiness.

Energy management is not the art of caffeinating ourselves to a level where we no longer feel the effects of fatigue. It is not measured by the number of hours you can keep your eyes open or the number of tasks you can juggle simultaneously. It's not about maintaining a 'hustle' culture or glorifying 'burnout' as a badge of honor. It is not the process of sacrificing your well-being at the altar of achievement.

Let's move the focus now to what energy management truly is. It's a holistic approach to life that respects the rhythmic cycle of expenditure and renewal. It's about finding a balance between exertion and rest, between giving and receiving. It's an understanding that our energy, much like the seasons, have an ebb and flow that should be honored and not resisted.

Energy management is an act of self-care and a form of self-respect. It's about recognizing your energy levels and adjusting your tasks to suit them. It is understanding that our energy isn't just physical, but also mental, emotional, and spiritual. It's about making time for nourishing activities that refill these energy tanks, such as meditation, exercise, art, music, reading, or simply spending time with loved ones.

At the heart of energy management lies a level of courage. It's the courage to admit when we're drained, and to say no when our energy levels are low. It's the courage of stepping away from the perpetual machine of 'doing,' and into the healing sanctuary of 'being'. It is the acceptance of our limits and the understanding that rest is not a luxury, but a necessity. It is not something you have to earn. It is something that you cannot function without.

Energy management is the deliberate choice to value yourself and your well-being. It means standing against a culture that often equates our worth with our productivity. It's about realizing that you are more than your output, and that replenishing your energy is not an act of indulgence but one of survival. It's about choosing to honor your needs, even when the world might not.

In essence, energy management is about embracing your humanness. It's the opportunity to practice grace and compassion with ourselves, to honor our need for rest, and to recharge in ways that truly serve us.

In our quest to manage our energy, we must learn to be intentional with ourselves by listening to the subtle cues our body and mind offer us. Energy management is not just an act; it is a lifestyle, and a deliberate choice to cultivate balance and prioritize well-being. Just like time, our energy is finite, and how we choose to expend and renew it will have lasting effects on not just you, but those who rely on you as well.

Energy Peaks and Valleys

Now that we understand the difference between time management and energy management, let's look at how we combine them to best benefit us. First, we need to start with two very important concepts.

1. Time is *not* a renewable resource.
2. Energy *is* a renewable resource.

We know this because we know we can't get more time in our day. Thinking about our buckets from the "Inspire," section, if our buckets are empty or just plain gone, we are not going to get them back through time management. It will only be through energy management, and as we use time as a tool to assist us with this, will we begin to get our buckets and "pixie dust" back.

To understand how best to use our energy, we need to be aware of its peaks and valleys. Using the form below, take a moment and think through your energy levels. Go through and use percentages, up to 100, to fill in your energy levels throughout the day. If you are asleep, just put 'sleeping'. Side note to my math geeks—this is not a zero-sum activity. You can have 100 percent in multiple areas. The numbers do not have to add up to 100 evenly.

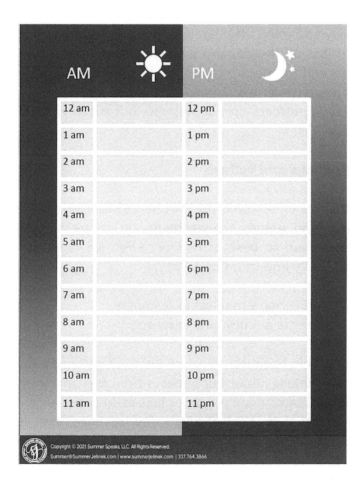

AM		PM	
12 am		12 pm	
1 am		1 pm	
2 am		2 pm	
3 am		3 pm	
4 am		4 pm	
5 am		5 pm	
6 am		6 pm	
7 am		7 pm	
8 am		8 pm	
9 am		9 pm	
10 am		10 pm	
11 am		11 pm	

Why do you think I had you do this exercise? Most of us have not spent any time thinking about our days and how we show up. We are so busy reacting to the world around us that we don't spend time figuring out how we want to show up. This activity helps us to understand our natural ebb and flow of energy, or our peaks and valleys.

As you look at your energy levels, answer the following questions:

1. When do you have the highest energy levels?
2. When do you have the lowest energy levels?
3. When do you tend to schedule your focus times?
4. What systems do you currently have in place to best take advantage of your energy highs and lows?
5. Now that you have this information, what systems do you need to put into place?

Understanding how our energy flows is the first step to effectively using time management as a resource to renew our energy.

One day I want to be able to take a nap every day. And I know when I would take that nap. It would be between 2:30 and 4. That time during the day is brutal for me. I am EXHAUSTED! In the morning, I have more energy. Making myself do something I don't want to do is much easier when I am not also fighting the urge to take a nap. Using what I know about my energy levels, I then use time management to arrange my day. Important meetings or tasks (like writing a book) happen in the morning when my energy is the highest. Administrative tasks, or tasks that don't require a lot of brain power, happen in the afternoon. We don't always have full control of our schedule. For example, if a client for an upcoming keynote can only meet at 3 PM, I am going to do that. I am also going to schedule a break 15 minutes before the call to take a quick walk outside and wake up a bit.

This is the power of combining energy management and time management. Knowing our energy levels, when they are full, when they are not, helps us build our day, as much as possible, around them.

Time Vacuums

During my career, I have been sent to a few time management classes. At the end of the class, I always remember feeling guilty about things, like I was wasting time, specifically with Netflix or social media. So I want to be very clear. This next section is not to cause any negative feelings. The purpose is to intentionally look at how you are using your time and determine if that is how you want to use it, or if you have simply fallen into a routine that is no longer working for you.

We can have activities, such as watching Netflix, looking at TikTok, or playing games, that bring us joy and allow our brains a chance to relax. Anytime a new *Bridgerton* season is out, I am going to spend my time binge-watching the entire season. That brings me a lot of joy. It is not wasted time because I am intentional about how I am using it, and I am not using it as an escape from other things I should be focusing on.

On the other hand, when I open up TikTok on my phone at night when I am laying in bed, I know even if my intention is to spend only five minutes on the app, I am going to spend at least an hour, if not more. So TikTok is not allowed in bed with me. That is something that I have to be intentional about as well.

Spending time doing things you enjoy, for no other reason than you enjoy them, is not a bad thing. Being intentional and not letting these things eat up all your time is what we are trying to do. We call things that eat up time like this, a time vacuum. We have lots of time vacuums, made up of some things we can avoid, and some things we can't. The first step in managing them is to look at where our time is going.

When we consider time vacuums, they are anything that causes you to lose time in a way that you are not happy with. Some examples could be social media, washing clothes, grocery shopping, TV, video games, commutes, meetings at work, or watching your kids play sports (hey...we are keeping it real). Not all of these will be a time vacuum for everyone. These are simply suggestions to get you going.

Find a piece of paper, a tablet, or anything you can write on. Spend five minutes writing anything that you consider to be a time vacuum.

Minimize, Maximize, Eliminate

Now that you have your list, spend time looking at the time vacuums.

Minimize

Are there time vacuums you can minimize and do less of? When I think of this, I think of not taking TikTok to bed with me. I still use TikTok, but I don't let it control me. I set boundaries around it that I can keep, so I can minimize it as a time vacuum, and use it as a source of relaxation instead. Another common example is video games. We don't have to get rid of them, but we can commit to no more than a half hour a day.

If you live with others and you are worried how they are going to react to you taking this time for yourself, offer to commit your half hour or so doing what you wish to do, and then ask what they want to do with their half hour. Then each of you help the other protect this time so you each are getting the time you need. This can be especially helpful if there are young kids involved. Looking at your list, put a minus (-) sign if there is a time vacuum you want to explore minimizing.

Maximize

Are there non-negotiable time vacuums you can modify with useful activities to make better use of the time? When I first started my keynote speaking business, I was in my car commuting for three hours a day. I used that time to listen to podcasts about becoming a better speaker, and on building a business. This time was a time vacuum that could be maximized. When I teach a, "Control Your Chaos," session, people have shared that they put on a podcast when they are cleaning, or they put on dance music and dance around the house, thereby getting some exercise and maximizing that time vacuum. Another person stopped going grocery shopping and instead moved to curbside pickup for her groceries. She spends the time she is now saving in a yoga class every week. After yoga, she goes to get her groceries. There are multiple ways to maximize a time vacuum. Looking at your list, put a plus (+) sign if there is a time vacuum you want to explore maximizing.

Eliminate

Finally, are there time vacuums that you need to eliminate? Is there something you are doing that no longer makes sense? Are there meetings at work you are attending simply because you were invited? You and others may not get actual value out of your attendance. Do you find yourself aimlessly watching TV, and later you don't remember what you were watching? Do you find yourself obsessively checking your email? If your computer makes a beep, do you immediately need to see who sent you a message? These are vacuums that take a significant amount of time every day. Look at your list and put an E next to a time vacuum if you want to explore eliminating it.

Think of it like this. Chances are you are pretty familiar with how much battery your phone currently has. You are probably also aware of when you get the dreaded red bars, meaning your phone is almost empty. What happens then? The race to find a phone charger has begun! The longer it takes to find the charger, the more anxious we get. If we put a third as much thought into our internal battery, and keeping it charged, as we do our phone batteries, we would be in a much better position to take care of ourselves and those that depend on us. Time is not a renewable resource, but energy is. Instead of focusing only on managing our time, it is helpful to focus on managing our energy as well.

CHAPTER 14

CHANNEL YOUR INNER ELSA AND LET IT GO

When I was in first grade, my father went to addiction treatment for alcoholism. He never touched a drop of alcohol from that point on. One of the side effects of growing up with a recovering alcoholic is that I spent a lot of time at Alcoholics Anonymous meetings. They would have open meetings where people could bring their loved ones. Normally, at these meetings, the kids would quickly find each other and we would create games to play. Even when playing, there was a moment in almost every meeting that would grab my attention. It is when the adults would say the serenity prayer, "Grant me the serenity to accept the things I cannot change, the courage to change the things I can, and the wisdom to know the difference."

As I got older, I came to notice that I would see my dad saying this when things were hard. I was curious because my dad is an atheist and doesn't believe in organized religion, so why was he saying a prayer? One day, in all of the brilliance of my sixteen year old self, I decided to ask him. He explained that words have power, and these words helped him to focus on the things he could control, instead of wasting time on the things he could not. To him, this made a big difference on how he responded to situations, and helped to keep him centered.

This has stuck with me as I have grown up. I would like to say that I only focus on what I can control, but that would be a lie. There are still times that I get into a battle with my daughter over eating her peas, or I truly believe that yelling at the jackass who just cut me off will influence their behavior. But it isn't as often as it used to be. I have found myself muttering the same words of my father when things get hard.

A big part of controlling your chaos is focusing on what you *can* control and just like Elsa from Frozen, letting the rest of it go. When we truly consider what we can control, it is actually pretty small.

Why do you think we spend so much time focusing on things outside of our sphere of control? A big part of it is that when we feel like we control things, we feel a sense of safety. When we lack a sense of control, we feel unsafe. If we explore it from a physiological perspective, controlling our environment means we are more likely to survive. That doesn't translate well into today's current environment though, which can cause us to begin focusing on many areas outside of our control. When we do that, we are pouring our energy down what I like to call the "black hole of drama." We start feeling a lack of control, so we begin focusing our energy on what is causing the lack of control, and we pour energy freely into the black hole. We assume we will feel better, but many times our anxiousness around the lack of control will simply grow, causing us to pour more energy, and so on. This is a vicious cycle that we find ourselves in.

When we consider leadership, it is ripe for a black hole of drama. We are trying to control our teams, ourselves, our families, our organizations, sometimes with no luck on any of the fronts. When you truly think about it, what is the only thing you can control?

That's right: You! We can influence, we can guide, but it is only ourselves that we can control.

Let's look at this in a visual way. In the book, 7 *Habits of Highly Effective People*, by Stephen Covey[1], the author introduced the circle of influence. There are two circles, the circle of influence, which is things we can control, and the circle of concern, which is things we can worry about, but have little to no control over.

The circle of concern can include global issues, economic conditions, the behavior of others, or any other external factors that you may not have direct control over. While you may be aware of these concerns, you cannot directly influence or change them.

The circle of influence represents the things that you can control or have the power to influence. This includes your thoughts, actions, choices, behaviors, attitudes, and relationships. It represents the areas of your life where you have direct control, and can make a difference.

When dealing with the circle of concern, individuals will find themselves more reactive to situations, and focusing on things outside of their control. Focusing on the circle of concern will begin to shrink your circle of influence and increase feelings of powerlessness and a diminished sense of control. An example of this is that annoying coworker that you have. You know the one. How much mental energy do you spend thinking through what you are going to say, or how you are going to let them know you are annoyed? If you are like most of us, you probably spend a fair amount of time on it. In this space, you are in the circle of concern. You are reactive to them, and what they do. You are pouring energy into the black hole of drama with no benefits. When we do this, it is because we are spending energy trying to control something, or someone, that cannot be controlled.

Reactive Focus
Negative energy reduces
the Circle of Influence

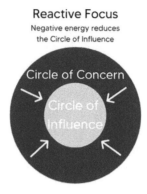

When dealing with the circle of influence, individuals are going to be more proactive, effectively using their energy where they have the biggest impact. When you are focusing on what you can actually impact and influence, your circle of influence will grow larger and you will have a stronger sense of control. Going back to the annoying coworker example, can we actually control them? No. Can you control how you react to them? Absolutely. You can't change their behavior, but you can change how you react to that behavior, and how much energy you are going to put into it.

Proactive Focus
Positive energy grows
the Circle of Influence

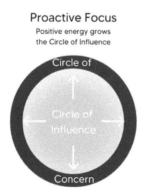

A great example of this is Kara Goldin, Founder and Former CEO of Hint Water. If you have not tried Hint Water, I cannot recommend it enough. Such a phenomenal product!

When Hint Water was first finding its legs, it was brought into Starbucks and provided a huge break. Starbucks told Kara's team that they would be happy if the Blackberry Hint sold 1.5 bottles per day across 6,000 stores. Very quickly, Hint started selling three bottles a day,which blew the expectations out of the water! So the Hint team started building up their supply so they could keep Starbucks supplied with enough product.

And then... a new executive at Starbucks, and a shift in direction came along, and even though Hint was exceeding expectations, the decision was made to pull it out of Starbucks. And to add insult to injury, there was only a week to do this. Hint was sitting on millions of dollars of inventory. Hint water isn't like regular water. It does not have an indefinite shelf life. Kara said during this time, she cried a lot. She wrote this down in her journal as a low point. She let herself feel the disappointment and frustration, and then she got to work. It just so happened that Amazon was building its direct-to-consumer grocery business. They emailed Kara and said they wanted to get her in on the new set but unfortunately they would need the product yesterday, so Hint was going to be added to the next set. Kara immediately focused on what she could control, which was to get the inventory that she had into the current set for Amazon. Due to having all of the back inventory, she was ready to go when this opportunity came.

When Kara was sharing this story, she shared such a valuable reminder, which was, "When you are in a bad situation, bad situations don't last forever."

Focusing on the areas you can control makes a huge difference in helping you to navigate out of these bad situations faster than if you focus on the areas you have no control over.

Let's break down the areas we have control over a little further.

- Our Actions - We have direct control over our actions. This includes our daily behaviors, how we choose to interact with others, and the decisions we make. We control what we eat, whether we exercise, how we perform our job, how we spend our free time, and so forth.
- Our Reactions - Although we don't control what happens to us, we control how we react. This involves our responses to both external events and internal feelings. When something unexpected occurs, or when someone else behaves in a certain way, we can choose our reaction.
- Our Attitude - Our attitude is under our control, whether positive or negative. Attitude is not necessarily about being overly optimistic or "fake." It's about maintaining a constructive outlook that can help us to better handle life's ups and downs.
- Our Effort - How much effort we put into our work, relationships, personal growth, and other areas of life is entirely up to us. While we can't control the outcomes, we can control the effort and dedication we put into trying to achieve them.

- Our Choices - We are constantly making choices, from the moment we wake up until we go to bed. These choices, large and small, shape the trajectory of our lives.
- Our Personal Growth - We decide how to invest in ourselves, whether through education, personal development, skills training, or by seeking feedback and learning from experiences.
- Our Words - We control what we say, when we say it, and how we say it. Words are powerful, and using them responsibly can have a significant impact on our relationships and experiences.

By understanding and acknowledging the areas of life we can control, we can become more empowered, more effective, and more resilient, especially in the face of adversity. We can grow our circle of influence and shrink our circle of concern.

Another aspect of, "Controlling Your Chaos," and focusing on your sphere of influence, is the ability to say *no*.

CHAPTER 15

WHY NICE PEOPLE HAVE MORE TIME

One of my favorite quotes is by Tony Blair, who states, "The art of leadership is saying no, not saying yes. It's very easy to say yes."[1]

This is so true. Many individuals I coach find themselves struggling with this tiny, two letter word, "No." They feel a variety of strong emotions around saying no, including guilt, shame, fear, and more. As we are a society of productivity, which means that we are a society of *yes*. We feel like the go-getter, the hustler, the person who does it all, is going to be the person that gets recognized. We can take it as a personal failure if we are unable to do everything that is being asked of us.

According to the New York Times,[2] human relationships are built on the rule of reciprocity. The rule of reciprocity states that we pay back what we have received from others. This is why we get so upset when we help someone out, and then when asking for their help, they say no. We have this unspoken, many times unconscious, expectation that they will do for us once we have done for them. This also explains why we have such a hard time saying no. Saying no feels threatening to us, like if we say no, we will lose out the next time we need assistance.

According to Synergy Health Programs,[4] "The power of saying no really comes down to the effects it has on our brain. When we say no more often, we shift the way our brain thinks and reacts to situations, allowing us more ability to make decisions for ourselves. This has a tremendous effect on our mental health, as it allows us to value ourselves more. It also helps us prioritize ourselves, and can even lead us to new opportunities that wouldn't have been achievable by saying yes."

For many individuals, saying no will never be easy, but it can get *easier*. As you begin this journey of being able to effectively say no, here is a model to assist you.

I created the N.I.C.E. model because as a good southern woman, I was taught by multiple generations of good southern women, that saying no and trying to balance my time is rude. So when this model was created, I wanted it to be understood that setting boundaries, including saying no, is not rude. There is a difference between being rude and being firm. The N.I.C.E. model will give you the tools to be firm and kind, but still maintain your boundaries.

N - Saying No
I - Acting with Intent
C - Getting Creative
E - Empowering Others

Saying No

Many times, how you say no will depend on who has asked you. Let's start with your leader or someone above you. If you are asked to take on something else and you are already feeling quite stretched, first ask yourself if this is something you want to do. Does it offer a growth opportunity? Is this a skill you want to learn? Will you have the opportunity to build your network? It is okay to ask questions to gain clarity when you are approached.

If you feel there is a strategic value in taking on this new task, but are not sure how to make it happen with your current workload, have a conversation with the person that asked you. In the conversation, share with the asker everything you are currently working on with approximate timelines. Ask them to help you prioritize so you can take on this extra project. It doesn't necessarily mean you have to give something up, it could mean that you adjust timelines on other projects. Many times our leaders have no clue what we are working on. They know results are being delivered, but not necessarily how they are being delivered. It can be educational for them to understand what your current workload looks like.

Now, if you feel there is no strategic value in the project, and it isn't something you want to take on, let them know that you wouldn't be the best person for the position, but you would love to ask around and see if there may be a better fit. If they are okay with that, ask around your network to find out who would be a good match, and who has the excitement and time to take it on. This way you are still involved in the solution without having to take on work that you don't have time for.

Now, if you are approached by a peer, you will do the same first steps of asking questions to gain clarity, thinking through if there is a strategic value, and determining if you want to move forward. If the answer is yes, then you will do the same thing for your peer. Share with them everything you are currently working on and ask if they would be able to assist in another area so you could open up time for this project with them.

Now, if you are considering the project and find that it isn't a fit, say no with compassion. It may look something like this:

"Thank you so much for considering me for this. I would love to assist, but unfortunately I do not have the ability to do so at this time. I know this isn't what you wanted to hear, but I don't want to say yes and then not be able to deliver for you."

And then STOP TALKING! Why? If you keep talking, you will talk yourself in circles until you have talked yourself into saying yes.

Sometimes you will have to say no to yourself as well. This comes back to intention. What do you want to do? What are you trying to create or influence? If what you are doing goes against that, it is time to say no to yourself as well. Start small and give yourself grace as you move through the 'no' journey. Many times, saying no to ourselves is the hardest.

Acting with Intent

The next step in the model is to act with intent. Being intentional has been a common theme throughout this book because it is so critical. Imagine you are on a sailboat. You are floating through the ocean and you respond based on what is happening around you. You will struggle knowing why and where you are going. But instead, if you have a clear direction, even when things come at you that you have to react to, you are able to get moving much quicker. This is the power of intentionality.

Prioritize

To do this in your day to day, the first step is to determine your priorities. What is important to you, what fills your bucket, what brings you energy? This could be family, work, hobbies, volunteering, faith—there are so many options. But if we don't know what our priorities are, how are we supposed to prioritize them?

Spend the next twenty minutes or so thinking through your priorities. A note about doing this: if everything is a priority, nothing is a priority. Your priorities will shift and that is okay. Right now, my main priority is finishing this book. My family is an extremely close second. When the book is complete, my priorities will shift again. Knowing where you are and what your priorities are, but also having grace with yourself as they shift, is an important part of controlling your chaos.

Do you have your priorities in mind? Great, read on. If you don't, go back and think through them again until you have an idea of what they are.

Once you have your priorities, look at your calendar and block out time to be specific around those priorities. Again, that time you have blocked may have to shift, but then you know you need to move it and it doesn't get lost.

At the beginning of every week, spend thirty minutes looking at the week ahead. Block time on your calendar that accurately reflects your week and activities. Are you going to have in person meetings that you will have to travel for? Block out the travel time. Need an agenda? Block out time to create one. Are you going to attend your kid's concert? Block out the time. Is there a singles' networking event you want to attend? Block out the time. We are more likely to respect time that we have blocked out, than to respect time we have in our heads.

At the end of every day, before you go home from work, spend ten minutes looking through your day. What did you accomplish that can be taken off of your list? What didn't get to happen today that needs to be shifted to tomorrow, or later in the week? What last minute thing has come up that you need to work into your schedule? Make sure and do this piece at the end of your day, that way everything you had to sort is still fresh in your mind.

Stay Focused Strategies

Here are a few time management techniques that you can use to help begin sorting your day.

Pomodoro Technique[4] - This method uses a timer to break your work into intervals, traditionally twenty-five minutes in length, separated by short breaks. Here are the basic steps:

- Pick a task you want to work on.
- Set a timer for twenty-five minutes (this is one "Pomodoro").
- Work on the task until the timer rings.
- Take a short break, around five minutes.
- Every four "Pomodoros," take a longer break, perhaps fifteen to thirty minutes.

The idea is that the timer creates a sense of urgency, which can make you more productive. Plus, regular breaks can help prevent fatigue and maintain a high level of mental agility.

Time Blocking - This technique involves dividing your day into blocks of time, each dedicated to accomplishing a specific task or group of tasks. It's a method of allocating a fixed, pre-scheduled time period for a planned activity. For example, you might block out 9:00 AM - 11:00 AM for focused work, 11:00 AM - 12:00 PM for meetings, and 1:00 PM - 3:00 PM for strategic planning. The key with time blocking is to be realistic about how much time tasks typically take, and to schedule yourself buffer time between tasks or blocks for unexpected challenges that may arise.

80/20 Rule (Pareto Principle)[5] - The Pareto Principle, named after the Italian economist Vilfredo Pareto, suggests that eighty percent of results come from twenty percent of efforts. In time management terms, this means focusing on tasks that yield the highest outcomes. You should identify and focus on the twenty percent of your tasks that are going to contribute to eighty percent of your results. It's a principle of prioritization and effectiveness over sheer hard work. This approach can help you focus your effort on what truly matters and eliminate or delegate less impactful tasks.

Each technique has its advantages and can be applied based on your own working style, the nature of the task, and the desired outcome. The most important thing is to experiment and find what methods work best for you to enhance your productivity.

Eliminate Distractions

The final step of acting with intent, is to eliminate distractions. One of the major changes you can make is to eliminate the sound of your devices. According to CNN[8], "Our smartphones are affecting our brains without us even being aware of it. When we hear the ping of an incoming text, social media update or email, our brains get a hit of dopamine, a chemical that leads to an increase in arousal, energizing the reward circuitry in our brains."

This makes it almost impossible to ignore the sound of an incoming email, text, or message. A research study at the University of California[6] found that it takes almost twenty-three minutes to get back on task after an interruption, like answering email or checking the ping from your phone. If you are using Microsoft Outlook and have not used the focus feature, I highly recommend learning how to turn it on. Do the same thing with 'do not disturb' on your phone. There are tools and resources to assist in eliminating distractions, you just have to be intentional about finding and using them.

Get Creative

The next step in the N.I.C.E model is to get creative. In the chapter on time and energy management, you went through and figured out your time vacuums, and then looked at ways to minimize, maximize and eliminate them. Sometimes in this process, we find really creative ways to utilize our time vacuums.

Consider this question: Do you currently have a time vacuum that you are holding onto because you think you *should*? Should is such a dangerous word. We put so much pressure on ourselves when we start thinking about all of the things we should, or should not do, be, say, or look like. It is high time we stop "shoulding" on ourselves!

An example from my world, is that I struggle to let go of the need to clean the house myself. I don't like the idea of hiring someone to do this for me. I struggled with this for quite awhile, but then came a day where I realized something had to give. Miles and I were fighting about the state of the house, but neither of us had the time or energy to do anything about it. So we talked, and decided to hire someone. The guilt was real, but so was the relief. Remember, guilt is a small price to pay for happiness. Since that experience, we have had someone come in twice a month. I know that this is a privilege and not everyone can afford it. The purpose of the story is to take off the filter of everything you *should* do, and start thinking through what you can get creative about to get some time back.

Empowering Others

The next step is empowering others, which has been woven throughout this book. The ability to empower others is such an amazing super power, but many leaders hesitate to do so. It could come from a lack of trust or inability to give up control, or the thought that you don't want to add more to someone else's plate. Either way, not empowering others is detrimental to your team, as well as to you.

Take a moment and think back to your favorite leader. When they came to you and asked for your assistance on something, how did you feel? Typically I get responses to this such as, valued, trusted, and proud. Clearly we know what it feels like when someone empowers us, so why do we fight so hard against empowering others?

One of the first steps is to look at what you and your team are currently doing and ask if these tasks belong to the right person. Do all of your tasks make sense? Is there something that feels like it should belong to another team? It may actually belong to them. 2020 sparked a massive wave of continuous layoffs that caused many employers to shuffle around tasks between far fewer employees. These shifts didn't always align with the task or skill set of the individuals. When companies began hiring people back in, a lot of these shifted tasks were overlooked or forgotten, and have since been with the unlucky team that inherited them. Have your team come up with the tasks they consistently do. Look through them together. Do these tasks still make sense? So much has changed and we were running in an effort to stay caught up. Now that we have a little bit of consistency back, we can be intentional about uncovering things that have not aged well in all of the changes over the past few years.

Tips for Empowerment

1. Get to know your people. To help individuals uncover their own power, it is helpful for you to know what their strengths are, the areas they want to grow and develop, or that they may be insecure in, the places you can push. and those you should stay away from. None of these will happen if you are only involved with your team when shit goes wrong. Spend one-on-one time with your team on a frequent basis, either in person or virtually.

2. Empower everyone, not just your favorites. Be aware of opportunities for bias to show. Make sure everyone gets time with you, not just the person you play pickleball with. Make sure everyone gets stretch assignments, not just the person who gives you travel tips. The Harvard Business Review reported that teams with inclusive leaders are 17 percent more likely to be high performing and 29 percent more likely to collaborate well.[7] Inclusivity isn't just a feel good concept, it is good for business and good for your team. When you role model inclusivity, your team will as well.

3. Be prepared when things go a different direction than you anticipated. When you empower others, they are going to do things differently from you, and that is okay. This is a lesson Miles taught me after our daughter was born. He was amazing in the hospital. I didn't change a single diaper. When we got home, he was hands-on the entire way. A few months after she was born, I noticed he started pulling back. I would have to ask for his help instead of him stepping in. I became furious very quickly. He was the father of our child and he needed to act like it. He looked at

me with a flat expression and said if he was going to get in trouble no matter what, he would rather get in trouble for not doing anything. I didn't expect this, and my anger dampened as my curiosity grew. He shared that every time he stepped in to help, I was telling him he was doing it wrong. Whether it was changing diapers, bathing her, feeding her, or rocking her to bed, I always insisted he do it my way. He got frustrated and stopped trying. That was the day that I realized there is more than just my way to get things done. If I want a partner, whether in my personal or professional life, I need to trust that partner to be able to deliver results even if the process looks different than what I would do.

Your employees will do things differently than you, and that is okay.

As you begin incorporating the N.I.C.E. model it is important to remember that it is like building muscle. It takes time and can feel awkward as you first start trying it. Try the different techniques to see what feels most natural, and more importantly, what feels like you will be able to consistently do. When you are incorporating change, success is made up in small, consistent steps, taken over time, not in one big giant leap.

CONCLUSION

It was a beautiful Orlando day. There were blue skies, it wasn't too hot, and there was just a touch of pixie dust in the air. I was working as a retail manager at Disney's Caribbean Beach resort. I walked backstage to the stockroom to grab something and I saw one of my Cast Members crying. I immediately got angry. Who was mean to her? Where were they? I was going to ensure they were never mean to another Cast Member again. She explained that no one had been mean to her, instead, there was a Guest who was having a bad day. She then looked at me, with tears in her eyes, and asked if we could do anything. I wasn't sure, but asked her to bring me to the Guest.

We walk out to the concierge desk, and there is the Guest. She is crying, the Concierge Cast Member is crying, and then my Cast Member sees them and starts crying too. I won't lie, tears have never been my strong suit. Internally, I was panicking a little bit.

My Cast Member introduced me to the Guest, who filled me in on what was happening.

It was her family's first time at Walt Disney World, and this was a once in a lifetime experience for them. They had been having an amazing experience, and decided to take a break from the parks and do some souvenir shopping at the local outlet mall. While they were shopping, someone cut open her backpack and took her phone and her camera.

As she was explaining this to me, all I could think about was that someone stole her memories. Stuff like this isn't supposed to happen at Disney. It always creates a feeling of helplessness and frustration when Cast Members hear of these moments. And in those moments of helplessness and frustration, we know a sprinkle of pixie dust tends to help.

I asked the Guest if they were going back to the parks, and she said no. Her family was at the hotel for a few more days, and then they were going home. I asked if they would be open to one more day at Magic Kingdom to see if we could work a little magic. She said yes and the concierge Cast Member gave her tickets for her and her family. While she was receiving these, I let her know she would be meeting Brian, a Disney Photopass leader, the next day at City Hall in Magic Kingdom at 9 AM. She thanked us and said she would be there.

I then walked to my office to call Brian and make sure he was working tomorrow morning at 9 AM. Thankfully he was, and he said he would take care of the Guest.

At 9 AM the next day, I get a text from Brian that read, "Guest is here, they will have a great time, call you later."

I anxiously awaited the news.

A few days later, we were able to catch up with Brian, myself, my Cast Member and the Concierge Cast Member so we could all hear what had happened with the family.

When the Guest arrived at Magic Kingdom, Brian assigned one of his Cast Members to go with the family and take pictures. He knew we couldn't replace the memories they had lost, but we could help capture the new ones.

At noon, he asked the Cast Member to bring the family to the castle. When the family arrived, Brian opened the door while explaining there were some special individuals who were anxious to meet the family. There, lined up along the wall, was every character that had been visiting with the park Guests that day. There was Cinderella, Mickey, Minnie, Peter Pan and so many more. The family spent the next hour taking pictures with all of the characters. Afterwards, the family went back out in the park, where their personal Cast Member continued taking pictures to document the day.

The best picture was one of Mom and Dad, holding hands, walking down Main Street, with the castle in front of them. It was a candid shot taken by the Cast Member that truly highlighted the magic of the day.

At around 9 PM, Brian figured the family had enough magic and brought them back to city hall where he presented them with photo albums with all of the best pictures. The ones from the characters had all been autographed. He also gave them a memory stick with the remainder of the pictures.

Mom, flipping through the photo albums, passed them to Dad and walked up to Brian and gave him a hug that was so tight, he couldn't breathe.

As Brian was sharing this story with me, I heard a very manly sniffle on the other end of the phone. My Cast and I were straight up bawling our eyes out. It was such an incredibly powerful and overwhelming moment to have been a part of.

It may be easy to think as you are reading this story, "It must be great to have Mickey Mouse in your back pocket. I can't do stuff like that. I don't have Mickey Mouse in my back pocket."

Sure, having Mickey Mouse does tend to make the pixie dust moments easier, but you see, the magic wasn't in Mickey, Minnie, Cinderella or any of the other characters.

The magic was in having leaders with the ability to **M**anage Themselves First, with employees fully **A**ligned on their Purpose, in an environment that allowed vulnerability and trust by having **G**alvanized Employees, with an entire team that was **I**nspired and had their **C**haos Controlled, so there was time to create this moment.

The *magic* was in every person that took part in that experience.

So what is your *magic*?

And what are you going to do with it?

Manage Yourself First

Align Your Purpose

Galvanize Your Employees

Inspire Yourself & Others

Control Your Chaos

ACKNOWLEDGMENTS

Thank you

To my mother and father for instilling in me a love of books and the knowledge that nothing is impossible if we want it enough. I always knew I wanted to write a book so I could see my mom go into the bookstore and buy it. Mom - You went home 6 months too early, but I know you are looking down and cheering me on.

To my big brother, Billy (AKA Ubi). I can't express how much it means to have you as a part of this journey. Thank you for the laughs, the support, the quiet understanding when the world gets too heavy, and for always keeping me humble.

To Mrs. Betty, thank you for letting me share your son and your name. And thank you for the perfect timing of encouragement. You always seem to know when I need it most.

To the amazing leaders that have shown me the magic along the way.

ACKNOWLEDGMENTS

Mrs. Floyd and Ms. Collum from back in the day, when it was so lonely. You showed me a leader can be a companion, guide, and friend.

Ben, for teaching me what it means to show up, even when it is hard.

Michele, you have always had my back, whether or not I deserved it.

Diane, you showed me that the best leaders don't always have to be the loudest in the room.

Dr. Bach, for not letting me give away my power, no matter how much I wanted to.

To the amazing Summer Speaks team, Katie, David, Alayna. I couldn't do this without you.

To my speaker family, Gary and so many others. Thank you for being there when I need a cheerleader, thought partner, or sympathetic shoulder.

To Courtney, for always being there for a quick call and brainstorm. For becoming my friend so many years ago, and finally, for stepping up when I needed you the most. We are on our way.

To Miles, you are the one person I can never put into words what you mean to me. It is too big. You are my person, forever and ever amen.

And to Levita, my little love. Thank you for being my cheering section. You are the best daughter a mom could ever wish for. To the moon, and the stars, and back (and back).

REFERENCES

Chapter 1

1. Dr. Susan Bach, personal conversation, March 2014
2. Dr. Rebekah Matheson, personal conversation, February 2023
3. Pendleton, B. (2017). The Elephant, The Rider, and the Path to Change in Healthcare. https://accelerate.uofuhealth.utah.edu/leadership/bob-pendleton-on-the-elephant-the-rider-and-change-in-health-care#:~:text=Jonathan%20Haidt%2C%20an%20NYU%20psychologist,of%20the%20need%20to%20change
4. Weintraub, K. (2018). Elephants are Very Scared of Bees. That Could Save Their Lives. https://www.nytimes.com/2018/01/26/science/bees-elephants-.html#:~:text=Of%20course%20a%20bee%27s%20stinger,And%20they%20hurt
5. Bennett, J. (2021). What if Instead of Calling People Out, We Called Them In? https://www.nytimes.com/2020/11/19/style/loretta-ross-smith-college-cancel-culture.html
6. Steffen, P. R., Hedges, D., & Matheson, R. (2022). The Brain Is Adaptive Not Triune: How the Brain Responds to Threat, Challenge, and Change. Frontiers in Psychiatry, 13, 802606. https://doi.org/10.3389/fpsyt.2022.802606

7. Segal, J., Smith, M. Robinson, L. (2023). Stress Symptoms, Signs, and Causes. https://www.helpguide.org/articles/stress/stress-symptoms-signs-and-causes.htm#:~:text=Your%20heart%20pounds%20faster%2C%20muscles,and%20your%20senses%20become%20sharper

8. Wilhelm, M. (2019). Why Giving In To Anger Makes Us Dumber. https://www.cumminsbhs.org/anger-makes-us-dumber/

9. Salovey, P., & Mayer, J. D. (1990). Emotional Intelligence. Imagination, Cognition and Personality, 9(3), 185-211. https://doi.org/10.2190/DUGG-P24E-52WK-6CDG

10. Goleman, D. (2007). Emotional Intelligence (10th ed.). Bantam Books.

11. Canfield, Jack. https://www.goodreads.com/author/quotes/35476.Jack_Canfield

Chapter 2

1. Chandler, N. (2023). What is the Butterfly Effect and How Do We Misunderstand It? https://science.howstuffworks.com/math-concepts/butterfly-effect.htm

2. Katie Fling, CEO of Katie Fling, personal conversation, August 2023

3. Frankl, Viktor E. (Viktor Emil), 1905-1997, author. Man's Search for Meaning : an Introduction to Logotherapy. Boston :Beacon Press, 1962.

4. Tina James, Retired Chief People Officer of H-E-B, personal conversation, February 2023

Chapter 3

1. Center for Creative Leadership. (2023). Authentic Leadership: What It Is, Why It Matters. https://www.ccl.org/articles/leading-effectively-articles/authenticity-1-idea-3-facts-5-tips/#:~:text=Authentic%20

leaders%20are%20those%20who,them%2C%20
and%20people%20ultimately%20matter

2. Jungmin Kang, CEO of snoopslimes.co, personal conversation, February 2023

3. Lee Hecht Harrison, Insights. https://www.lhh.com/ca/en/organizations/article-listing/?language=en&sort=newestfirst

4. Brene' Brown. Dare to Lead Hub. https://brenebrown.com/hubs/dare-to-lead/

Chapter 4

1. Glassdoor. (2023). Best Places to Work 2023. https://www.glassdoor.com/Award/Best-Places-to-Work-LST_KQ0,19.htm

2. Greater Good Magazine. https://greatergood.berkeley.edu/topic/purpose/definition

3. Duarte, N. (November 2011). The Secret Structure of Great Talks. Ted Conferences. https://www.ted.com/talks/nancy_duarte_the_secret_structure_of_great_talks?language=en

4. Collins, J. (2001). Good to great. Random House Business Books.

5. Berger, M. (2023). Does more money correlate with greater happiness? https://penntoday.upenn.edu/news/does-more-money-correlate-greater-happiness-Penn-Princeton-research#:~:text=Foundational%20work%20published%20in%202010,leveled%20off%20and%20happiness%20plateaued

6. Achor, S., Reece, A., Kellerman, G., Robichaux, A. (2018). 9 out of 10 People are Willing to Earn Less Money to Do More Meaningful Work. https://hbr.org/2018/11/9-out-of-10-people-are-willing-to-earn-less-money-to-do-more-meaningful-work

7. Tyrone Frost, personal communication, March 2023

8. Vaccaro, A. (2014). How a Sense of Purpose Boosts Engagement. https://www.inc.com/adam-vaccaro/purpose-employee-engagement.html

9. The Walt Disney Company. About the Walt Disney Company. https://thewaltdisneycompany.com/about/#:~:text=Our%20Mission,the%20world%27s%20premier%20entertainment%20company

10. Sullivan, J. (2017). Mock Boot Camp Gives USAA Employees a Taste of Military, Pushups Included. https://sanantonioreport.org/mock-boot-camp-gives-usaa-employees-a-taste-of-military-pushups-included/

11. Kukulski, M. (2020) Facebook. https://www.facebook.com/atcmemesofficial/posts/keepdeanhttpswwwfacebookcom100038664990133posts212439253388240dn/2668334406610033/

12. Castrillon, C. (2019). Why Purpose is the New Competitive Advantage. https://www.forbes.com/sites/carolinecastrillon/2019/04/28/why-purpose-is-the-new-competitive-advantage/?sh=69159ddd711f

13. Cockerell, L. (2022). Hiring and Retaining the Right Employees.https://www.leecockerell.com/hiring-and-retaining-the-right-employees/

Chapter 6

1. Brown, B. (2012). Vulnerability is the birthplace of innovation. Ted Conferences. https://blog.ted.com/vulnerability-is-the-birthplace-of-innovation-creativity-and-change-brene-brown-at-ted2012/

2. Cengage Group. (2022). What's Driving the Great Resignation? Pay, Burnout and Stalled Career Growth, According to Cengage Group Research. https://www.prnewswire.com/news-releases/

whats-driving-the-great-resignation-pay-burnout-and-stalled-career-growth-according-to-cengage-group-research-301464702.html#:~:text=Employers%20must%20prioritize%20professional%20development,longer%20growing%20in%20their%20positions

Chapter 7

1. Gallo, A. (2023). What is Psychological Safety? https://hbr.org/2023/02/what-is-psychological-safety#:~:text=Team%20psychological%20safety%20is%20a,it%27s%20felt%20permission%20for%20candor.%E2%80%9D

2. Hastwell, C. (2023). What is Psychological Safety in the Workplace? How Leaders Can Build Psychologically Safe Workplaces. https://www.greatplacetowork.com/resources/blog/psychological-safety-workplace

3. Duhigg, C. (2016). What Google Learned From Its Quest to Build the Perfect Team. https://www.nytimes.com/2016/02/28/magazine/what-google-learned-from-its-quest-to-build-the-perfect-team.html?_r=0

4. Crookes, L. (2021). What's In a Name - Addressing Name Bias in Recruitment. https://www.linkedin.com/pulse/whats-name-addressing-bias-recruitment-lucy-crookes/

5. Johns, B.T., Dye, M. Gender bias at scale: Evidence from the usage of personal names. Behav Res 51, 1601–1618 (2019). https://doi.org/10.3758/s13428-019-01234-0

6. Nikolopoulou, K. (2023). What is Affinity Bias - Definitions and Examples. https://www.scribbr.com/research-bias/affinity-bias/#:~:text=Affinity%20bias%20is%20the%20tendency,or%20look%20different%20to%20us

Chapter 8

1. Thiel, C., Bonner, J., Bush, J., Welsh, D., Garud, N. (2022). Monitoring Employees Makes Them More Likely to Break Rules. https://hbr.org/2022/06/monitoring-employees-makes-them-more-likely-to-break-rules

Chapter 9

1. Business Standard. (2021) https://www.business-standard.com/content/specials/success-is-not-final-failure-is-not-fatal-it-is-the-courage-to-continue-that-counts-winston-churchill-121042300664_1.html
2. The Henry Ford. https://www.thehenryford.org/collections-and-research/digital-resources/popular-topics/henry-ford-quotes/
3. Salama, F. (2023). Feedback Sandwich for Effective Communication. https://www.makingbusinessmatter.co.uk/feedback-sandwich/#:~:text=Who%20Invented%20the%20Feedback%20Sandwich,remarks%20between%20layers%20of%20praise
4. Schwarz, R. (2013). The "Sandwich Approach" Undermines Your Feedback. https://hbr.org/2013/04/the-sandwich-approach-undermin#:~:text=If%20you%20give%20a%20feedback,believing%20it%20is%20not%20genuine
5. Brown, B. (2018). Clear is Kind. Unclear is Unkind. https://brenebrown.com/articles/2018/10/15/clear-is-kind-unclear-is-unkind/
6. Leading Effectively Staff. The Center for Creative Leadership. (2022). https://www.ccl.org/articles/leading-effectively-articles/closing-the-gap-between-intent-vs-impact-sbii/

Chapter 10

1. Bjelland, J. (2019). How Overgiving Leads to Resentment. https://community.thriveglobal.com/how-overgiving-leads-to-resentment/
2. Popken, B. (2011). Walmart Declutters Aisles Per Customers' Request, Then Loses $1.85 Billion in Sales. https://consumerist.com/2011/04/18/walmart-declutters-aisles-per-customer-request-then-loses-185-billion-in-sales/
3. Friedman, S. (2014). What Successful Work and Life Integration Looks Like. https://hbr.org/2014/10/what-successful-work-and-life-integration-looks-like
4. The Greater Good Science Center. (2018). The Science of Gratitude. https://ggsc.berkeley.edu/images/uploads/GGSC-JTF_White_Paper-Gratitude-FINAL.pdf
5. Stewart, D. (2017). Gratitude creates gratitude. https://www.mayoclinichealthsystem.org/hometown-health/speaking-of-health/gratitude-creates-gratitude
6. Barnes, C. (2016). Research: Sleep-Deprives Leaders Are Less Inspiring. https://hbr.org/2016/06/research-sleep-deprived-leaders-are-less-inspiring#:~:text=In%20sum%2C%20we%20found%20evidence,are%20more%20difficult%20to%20inspire

Chapter 11

1. Kenrick DT, Griskevicius V, Neuberg SL, Schaller M. Renovating the pyramid of needs: Contemporary extensions built upon ancient foundations. Perspect Psychol Sci. 2010;5(3):292-314. doi:10.1177/1745691610369469
2. Melissa Adams, personal conversation, March 2023.
3. Bauer, T. (2019). How did Dostoevsky say you destroy a prisoner psychologically? https://thecontextofthings.com/2019/01/03/how-did-dostoevsky-say-you-destroy-a-prisoner-psychologically/

Chapter 12

1. Center for Self-Determination Theory. https://selfdeterminationtheory.org/theory/
2. Duhigg, C. (2016). What Google Learned From Its Quest to Build the Perfect Team. https://www.nytimes.com/2016/02/28/magazine/what-google-learned-from-its-quest-to-build-the-perfect-team.html?_r=0

Chapter 14

1. Covey, S. R. (2013). The 7 habits of highly effective people: Powerful lessons in personal change. Simon & Schuster

Chapter 15

1. Parrish, S. (2015). A Successful Leader Has to Learn to Say No. https://time.com/3944852/successful-leader-say-no/
2. Wong, K. (2017). Why You Should Learn to Say 'No' More Often. https://www.nytimes.com/2017/05/08/smarter-living/why-you-should-learn-to-say-no-more-often.html
3. Synergy Health Programs. (2022). The Power of No: Wgt Satubg "No" is Important. https://synergyhealthprograms.com/why-saying-no-is-important/#:~:text=The%20power%20of%20saying%20no,us%20to%20value%20ourselves%20more
4. Scroggs, L. The Pomodoro Technique. https://todoist.com/productivity-methods/pomodoro-technique
5. The Investopedia Team. (2022). What is the Pareto Principle - aka the Pareto Rule or 80/20 Rule? https://www.investopedia.com/terms/p/paretoprinciple.asp
6. Mark, G., Gonzalez, V., Harris, J. (2005). No Task Left Behind? Examining the Nature of Fragmented Work. https://ics.uci.edu/~gmark/CHI2005.pdf

7. Bourke, J., Titus, A. (2019). Why Inclusive Leaders Are Good for Organizations, and How to Become One. https://hbr.org/2019/03/why-inclusive-leaders-are-good-for-organizations-and-how-to-become-one

8. Wallace, K., (2016). Driving While Distracted. Why We Can't Ignore the Pings. https://www.cnn.com/2016/08/03/health/distracted-driving-addiction-brain-impact/index.html